*A***FALCON**GUIDE®

How to Climb Series

Coaching Climbing

A Complete Program for Coaching
Youth Climbing for High Performance and Safety

Michelle Hurni

A FALCON GUIDE®

Text design: Linda Loiewski
Illustrations: Martha Morris

Library of Congress Cataloging-in-Publication Data
Hurni, Michelle.
   Coaching climbing : a complete program for coaching youth climbing for high performance and safety / Michelle Hurni.-- 1st ed.
     p. cm.
   Includes index.
   ISBN 0-7627-2534-6
   1. Rock climbing for children--Coaching. 2. Climbing gyms. I. Title.

GV200.23.C35 H87 2003
796.52'23--dc21

2002024578

Manufactured in the United States of America
First Edition/First Printing

CONTENTS

Acknowledgments

I would like to extend a huge thank-you to Rob Candelaria of CATS in Boulder, Colorado, for every time he pushed me beyond my "limits" and for all the training advice and time he gave me over the years.

Another big thank-you goes out to the U.S. Climbing Team, for all the trainers who donated their time over the years and for all the training sessions where I was able to absorb multitudes of training ideas.

And perhaps one of the biggest thank-yous goes to my partners over the years—all of them were of enormous help to my climbing ability, from those in Illinois to all the partners I was able to hook up with around the country. I would like to raise my glass in a special big THANK-YOU to Karin Budding and Kim Knuth for all those years when we didn't know how good we had it until it was over.

My heartfelt thanks to the unbelievable support I continue to receive from Marmot, Boreal, Metolius, Aloe Up, and everyone at Falcon.

This book is dedicated to Garrett and George.

Introduction

Coaching Climbing: A Complete Program for Coaching Youth Climbing for High Performance and Safety is ideal for personal coaches who are teaching young climbers to improve their skill—whether it is to compete, improve personal climbing abilities, or to crank hard outside. All of these objectives have one common thread that links these kids together: improving technique to become a better climber.

How to Use This Guide

"Climbing is 5 percent technique and 95 percent mental."

This book is designed primarily to use during training sessions, but much of coaching is working with the mindset of the climber, which I also address.

As a personal trainer for a young climber, you will need to study this book ahead of time to learn ways to keep your students motivated. A session should be planned with no more than two exercises that can be implemented during practice. Although some of the exercises can be used together, most need to be performed alone. I find that it works best to expect that only one or two exercises will be used during a training session. Don't give your students too much and then have to rush through the exercises.

In this book I address most issues involved in training a young climber. Other topics I just touch upon, as there is already an abundance of material about these subjects elsewhere (see the Resources section of the Appendix). As a coach, you will need these additional resources to supplement information in this book.

At times it may sound as though I am being harsh or strict about the training process. This is sometimes necessary to ensure that your students are receiving proper training. You are there to help them improve—if they are not, you may both be wasting your time. After awhile, you will know what works for your individual climbers. The important thing to remember is that each concept should be grasped by your student before moving on to the next activity. Whether you do it with a strict hand or a gentle urging, the climber is there to learn—and you are the most important tool available to him.

Why Coach a Young Climber?

You definitely will not be coaching for a prominent salary, so there must be other reasons. If you are volunteering your time—more power to your energy and devotion!

The main reason for coaching a young climber is to help her succeed. Success comes from sticking with climbing—improving and having fun. As the coach, you will be instrumental in that success.

As a personal coach, I have found that the payment for this service varies drastically from town to town. Generally speaking, if you are able to, set up a fee schedule that works for you. My preferred method is typically a set fee of $25 to $50 per session per student for personal (one-on-one) training. I consider a "session" as long as it takes to get my student the best workout possible—usually two to three hours at a bouldering gym working on power training or three to four hours in a climbing gym working on routes and endurance. If you are coaching more than one student at a time, you can divide this fee among them, with a slight increase. Most of my students will only train one day a week with me at those rates, but if your students are also part of a team or are self-motivated to carry out your program outside the sessions, then one day of personal training is probably sufficient. Remember, your time is valuable; you need to make sure you will not quit if you don't have that monetary reward.

Young climbers often need a structured program so that they are not just floundering in the climbing gym. Your primary job will be to keep your student from getting bored and giving up the sport. If a climber shows up at the gym unmotivated or unwilling to push, you will need to decide whether to change your plan of action or to stay with what you had scheduled for the day. If I have a student show up lacking motivation, I will often change my plan to her favorite type of climbing so that she will at least want to climb and get in a good workout.

When the motivation or enjoyment returns, you may be able to work back into what you had scheduled for the session. The student's lack of motivation will need to be addressed during the training session so that it doesn't happen on a regular basis. Attitudes will be discussed later in this chapter.

Most climbers go through a period of time—a day, a week, a month, even up to a year—where they do not feel like climbing. Sometimes time off from climbing is the answer; then the motivation and love for the sport will return. If a climber is not motivated, she will not push hard enough to improve. If a climber takes a break, his mind can clear; he will probably miss climbing and want to do it again—stronger than before because his body has had a chance to fully recover from the abuse of climbing.

Most coaches tend to be parents, generously donating their time to the activity their child has chosen. Some parents know nothing about climbing, yet they want to be able to help their child improve her climbing performance. In most locations there are coaches at the local climbing gym, but sometimes there is no coach available and parents must be their child's personal trainer. This book gives coaches of all types a broad base for developing a training program for individual climbers, even if they don't have a climbing background.

Attitudes

"Life is not fair—get used to it."
—Bill Gates

Attitudes among young climbers range from bored to ambitious. No matter what type of student you are coaching, you will need to keep her motivated, which can be a challenge. I have worked with climbers who are bored and unmotivated but still want to be good climbers. The problem with these types of students is getting them motivated enough to actually want to climb. You will need to get the real answer from these students as to their motivation for success. For example, if a student is motivated by peer acceptance, deal with that as a motivating factor for him. For some climbers it is not the climbing that is the reward but the accolades that come with success.

My favorite students are those who don't question what I ask them to do, no matter how silly the exercise may seem to them. These are the climbers who will improve the quickest——those who will work hard for what they want to achieve.

Of course, it is also important to give those climbers a reason for what they are doing so that the entire process (including thoughts) is a part of the exercise. Determine which students want to work to succeed. Motivated climbers will be the easy ones. The others will need to be cajoled, encouraged, and cracked down on so that they will climb to the utmost of their ability. Structured programs, with little room for "playtime" are best for the unmotivated climbers. As these students see improvement, they will probably want to work harder to reach their goals.

Be sure to lay down the rules from the beginning. You are the coach and probably know a lot better than your students what will work for them!

Parents

By coaching young kids, you will (by default) be dealing with their parents. You may have parents who want their children to succeed and win at all costs. One thing you may have to discuss with these parents is the fact that climbing—as a sport—is very different from almost every other athletic activity out there.

Climbing is a very internal activity, and most kids will judge themselves on their own merits, not on how they compare with others in the gym. Almost every climber in the gym looks around, sees what others are able to accomplish, and tries a little harder based on those observations. Climbing is less of a "game" with winners and losers and more of a "sport" of development.

If you have parents who do not understand climbing, try to educate them. Let them know what is going on in your coaching sessions. Ask them to sit in on a session so that they can watch their child struggle—and succeed.

Encourage parents to keep climbing in perspective. Unfortunately, there are not currently a lot of long-term opportunities for climbers—scholarships are pretty well nonexistent, high-paying jobs are in the minority, and there are not enough competitions to make a living. Climbing is a great physical and mental activity for kids, and perhaps parents should view it as such.

Where to Start

If you are coaching for the first time, there will be many decisions to make, all of which will play a vital part in your success. If you are starting with a complete beginner climber, your job will be a lot different than if you are coaching an experienced climber who has already worked on technique.

Any age is a good age to start climbing! Ian Spencer-Green bouldering at age eight. Photo: Stewart Green

If you are working with a complete beginner, you will need to start with the basics of climbing: belay techniques, putting on a harness, picking out shoes, tying into the rope, etc. The basics can be found in instructional books and are also touched upon in Chapter 2.

Coaching an experienced climber will be a slightly different job. An experienced or even intermediate level climber may pose a challenge if she has developed bad habits that you will have to work to correct. Often it's harder to correct bad habits than it is to teach new techniques.

This section will make your job a little easier—just follow the outlined steps.

• First determine what type of program you are going to use (see "Types of Coaching," next section).

• Determine what your student's goals are.

- Establish the number of days a week you will be able to commit to your student and then determine how many more days that student needs to climb outside of those sessions.

- Decide if you need to prepare for a competition season.

- Find out what the local climbing gym is willing to contribute: extra (open gym) hours for you to train, funding for traveling to events, sponsorship, a discount for your student to train in the gym, etc.

- Decide if you will work one-on-one with a student or if you will allow other climbers to join your practice sessions. This is an important decision factor, as even one other student can change the dynamics of the session. On the other hand, working with two students at a time can help push each student beyond his own expected ability level.

- Write down your own personal goals and reasons for coaching, and then evaluate whether you are doing it for the right reasons. Your student must be your primary concern.

- When starting a coaching program, it's a good idea to network with other coaches. Currently, there is no established certification program, so meeting other coaches can help when you need advice or have questions. You can find an extensive list of gyms in the back of *Climbing* and *Rock & Ice* magazines. Call the gyms in your area to get the names of coaches who teach there. Another resource is the Climbing Gym Association, which is a subgroup of the Outdoor Industry Association (OIA).

Types of Coaching

The type of program you set up for your student needs to be based on what that student's goals are. Goals can range from competitive climbing (competitions) to climbing for fun on a regular basis. Sometimes a student will have a variety of objectives; you need to determine how/if those objectives can be met. One student may not want to compete but may want to climb hard outside, using the gym just to train. A second climber may only want to compete, so the schedule needs to be set up around the competition season. Another may just be there to climb for fun and to learn how. With all of these different objectives, it can be difficult to train more than one climber during a session, and you may have to have one-on-one sessions with your students.

Once you determine what type of program your student needs, you can then decide on a schedule to meet those objectives (see "The Schedule" and "Setting Goals" in Chapter 3).

TYPES OF CLIMBING PROGRAMS TO CHOOSE FROM

1. **Competitive:** traveling to compete on either a local or national competition schedule

2. **Beginner/instructional:** consisting of a beginner to intermediate climber committed to learning the sport and improving his technique

3. **Training:** working with a climber who actually wants to train hard inside to climb hard outside

4. **Bouldering:** working on bouldering instead of climbing with ropes—for a climber wishing to boulder either indoors or outdoors

5. **Roped climbing:** working with a student to improve her roped climbing skills, either sport or traditional climbing, indoors or outdoors

The Gym

Each commercial climbing gym is going to be unique as to what it will make available to you as a coach. This will need to be discussed in detail with the gym owner/manager. The list below can give you an idea of things that need to be established before you begin coaching students.

- Will you and your student need to join the gym to use it for training sessions?

- Will the gym help coordinate such activities as belaying and route setting for your needs?

- Is it possible to have access to the gym when it is closed to the general public?

- Will you need to do projects (cleaning up, helping belay during introduction classes, setting routes, etc.) for the gym to retain your coaching privileges?

- Will the gym receive a percentage of your coaching fees? This is very common if you are working at a gym that helps coordinate your schedule with your students, similar to a personal trainer at a health club.

- Is there any way for the gym to help out if a student is positively unable to pay your coaching fees, such as a scholarship program?

- What are the most convenient days for you to use the gym? Low use times are best for all involved so that there are more routes available without waiting for gym members to finish climbs.

Remember, the climbing gym and gym employees are some of your most valuable resources; it's important to retain a good working relationship with them.

PERSONAL/PRIVATE GYM

If you are lucky enough to have a personal or private gym at your disposal, you have an advantage. A personal gym is typically for private use—sometimes in a basement or garage—and should allow more flexibility in your schedule and coaching practice, although you may have to deal with heavy-use times by other climbers using the gym.

John Sherman surveying the bouldering gym Rod Willard built in Estes Park.
Photo: Rod Willard

If using a private gym, you will need to talk to the owner about what you can and cannot do. One of the paramount benefits of a private gym is being able to set and mark problems for your student. This will make each session more exciting, as you can make up new problems/routes each week; your student will not get bored with what is up on the wall. You may also have the ability to move holds around to positions that work for specific exercises, but speak with the gym owner first!

Chapter 1: **Gym Climbing 101**

So you don't climb? You don't know much about climbing? That's okay, you can still coach. Your first step will be to understand the lingo involved in the world of climbing (see the Glossary in the Appendix). The second step is to learn the basics of climbing: equipment, techniques, grades, etc. Climbing is not a traditional team sport. It is closer to gymnastics or dance than basketball or soccer. Learning to climb is training the body, learning individual movement, and educating the mind.

If you have previous coaching or teaching experience and a basic grasp of the concept of climbing, you can begin to coach. There are plenty of exercises and activities in later chapters to keep your students occupied, and once you have used a few, you can create some of your own.

This chapter is here to answer all the questions you, as a nonclimber, potential coach, or parent, need answers to. Broken down into four sections—Climbing, Coaching, Safety, and Setting Problems and Routes—this chapter should answer all of your basic climbing questions.

Climbing

HOW MANY STUDENTS SHOULD BE IN A GROUP/TEAM?

If you are not using a one-on-one ratio for coaching, there is a lot of leeway in how many kids can be in a group or team. Personally, I feel the smaller the group the better. This is not to be lazy but to give the kids more individual coaching time and personal attention. In a team or group situation, I would recommend no more than six to eight kids to one adult. Any more than that and the coach spends too much time giving basic instruction and averting problems rather than coaching the needs of each student. With only a couple of hours in the gym, you need to be efficient with your coaching time to avoid running from student to student putting out fires. If the kids are younger than twelve, each child should have an adult or parent in the gym for belaying purposes.

If you end up with a large team, you can have an assistant coach at each session so that you can divide the group into more manageable numbers.

WHAT EQUIPMENT DO MY STUDENTS NEED?

The list of equipment needed for climbing indoors is basic: harness, shoes, chalk bag/chalk, belay device, and locking carabiner for use with the belay device. For climbing outdoors, the list grows substantially (as outlined in Chapter 17). All of the items listed below are available to rent from most climbing gyms, but if a student is going to be climbing often (more than twice a week), it will probably be financially advantageous to purchase these items.

- **Harness:** The first thing to consider when shopping for a harness is the comfort of the leg loops and waist belt, which is especially important when hanging or lowering off a climb. A harness may be comfortable while standing on the ground, but think about being in the harness for numerous hours

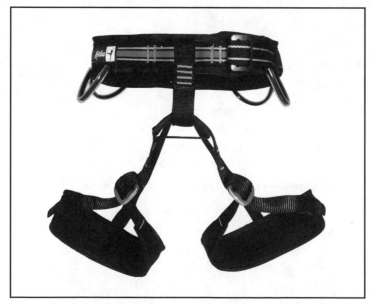

The Freedom harness from Metolius is a simple harness for indoor and outdoor sport climbing. Photo: Metolius

while belaying, being lowered, or just plain hanging while working out moves. You don't want a harness that will restrict movement in any way while climbing, but you do want it to be snug enough that it does not ride up or shift during a fall or while being lowered. A basic sport climbing harness is all that is needed for climbing in a gym. Don't worry about all the accessories that are available with more expensive models. A harness will cost between $45 and $85 for the 2003 season. You should probably not purchase a used harness without knowing its detailed history. Webbing can be worn or abused, and it may not be obvious to an inexperienced eye. As long as it is not outgrown, a harness will last for many years.

• **Shoes:** Shoes are another personal item that is nice to own rather than rent. Comfort and fit are paramount, and climbing shoes should be comfortably

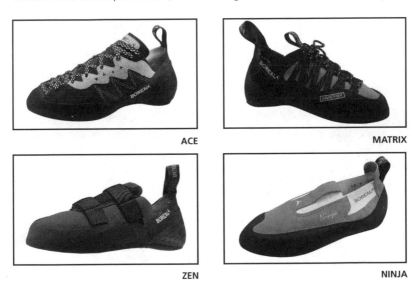

ACE   MATRIX

ZEN   NINJA

There are different shoes for different types of climbing. The Ace is a great outdoor crack climbing shoe while the Matrix is excellent for technical sport climbing. The Zen and Ninja are Velcro and slip-ons, easy to use indoors.
Photo: Boreal

tight without causing pain. There are numerous types available: Some are better for gyms, others are softer for sport climbing, and some are stiffer for traditional climbing. A slipper, shoe without laces, is great for gym climbing as it can be easily removed when not climbing; it typically has a very soft sole for standing on small holds. A lace-up shoe can also be worn in the gym, but make sure the sole is not so stiff that you can't turn it with your hands.

A stiff shoe is great for crack climbing outdoors but will not have as much sensitivity for indoor/artificial rock climbing. Be sure the shoe is snug; otherwise the foot can slide around inside and cause the climber to be off balance. Once a year *Rock & Ice* and *Climbing* magazines review new and existing shoes on the market. New climbing shoes will run $85 to $145. Beginner climbers tend to wear out the rubber on the base of the shoe in the toe area and shoes can be resoled for $35 to $45. Understanding that children outgrow shoes and that $85 to $145 is a significant investment, I still do not recommend buying shoes that they will "grow into." Instead buy used and resell the shoes as they are outgrown. When purchasing used shoes, be aware of the rubber on the bottom. If the rubber on the upper/front of the toe is worn through, the shoes will need to be resoled. A typical pair of shoes for a beginner climber may last one to two years before needing to be resoled. There are many climbing shoe companies to choose from, with Boreal, LaSportiva, and Five.Ten being the most popular.

- **Chalk bag:** A chalk bag is a simple and inexpensive yet necessary accessory. There are many chalk bag styles, and choosing one is strictly personal preference. Bags range in size from fingertip (extremely small) to entire hand size. For climbing in a gym, it is not necessary to chalk up the entire hand; generally only the fingertips and sometimes the palm are sufficient.

A chalk bag is a personal choice. Photo: Metolius

Chalk bags range in price from around $15 to $25. A belt is also necessary to attach the chalk bag to the body; webbing with a quick-release buckle costs about $6.00. Some people attach their chalk bag to their harness with a carabiner, but that doesn't allow the chalk bag to lay flat against the body and the climber must fish around to dip in.

- **Chalk:** Gymnastics chalk is necessary if a climber's hands sweat because it will dry off the sweat and make the hands stick to holds better. The biggest choice is whether to use a chalk ball or loose chalk. Loose chalk gets in the air and can spill, and some gyms don't allow its use. A chalk ball (small nylon refillable pouch) does not spill or create such a mess. The downside to a chalk ball is you can't just "dip" into the bag and get chalk; you have to squeeze the ball to get it on the fingers.

The Metolius BRD is an excellent choice for a belay device. Photo: Metolius

- **Belay device:** A belay device is another personal preference item, but there are a couple of notes of caution, especially for kids. Regular belay devices by Trango, Jaws & Pyramid, or Metolius BRD are good choices and cost around $20. A figure-8 (available from many climbing companies) is a rappelling device, not a belay device, although a lot of people use it as such. A figure-8 should not be used in the gym for belaying. It kinks the ropes and is not as easy to control as a belay device, especially for younger climbers. I personally love my Petzl Grigri but must provide a quick note of caution on this self-locking, foolproof device. One problem with the Grigri is that it can be used incorrectly (rope threaded through backward) and become totally ineffectual. Another problem is that for small climbers the rope must be force fed for a climber to be lowered; the third problem is the expense—around $70.

- **Locking carabiner:** This is usually a simple purchase, costing from $10 to $25. A locking carabiner is necessary for attaching the belay device to the harness and should remain locked any time the belay device is in use. There are numerous choices for locking carabiners: Some lock themselves, others have screw locks, and still others have twist locks. Locking biners are personal preference, and you should purchase whichever is the easiest for you to operate.

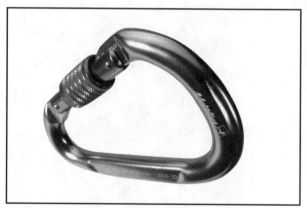

The large screw-locking carabiner from Metolius is easy to get around both the leg loops and waist belt of the harness. Photo: Metolius

WHEN SHOULD MY STUDENT PURCHASE EQUIPMENT?

If your student decides to climb on a regular basis (more than twice a week), and sticks with it for more than one season, chances are he is better off buying rather than renting equipment. Traveling to compete in competitions is another good reason to purchase equipment so that your student can always be assured of having gear that fits. You don't want to get to a gym for a competition and find that she doesn't have the proper size shoes!

Equipment can be purchased from your local gym's pro shop; from any major outdoor store, such as Galyan's or REI; or from numerous on-line climbing stores.

WHAT IS TOPROPING?

Toproping (TR) is when the rope runs from the belayer to the top of the wall and then down to the climber. In some gyms a toprope is attached to the top of the wall with carabiners and is typically fixed in place and not taken down. Other gyms have a metal bar with the rope wrapped around it for friction. In a gym situation, most ropes are hanging from the ceiling, scattered throughout the gym at 5- to 10-foot intervals. Topropes allow a climber to walk up to the base of the wall, tie in and climb a route to the top, and then be lowered to the ground by their belayer.

Focused on footwork and body tension, Erin Axtell topropes a steep route.
Photo: Craig Axtell

WHAT IS LEAD CLIMBING?

Lead climbing, or leading, is the next step up from toproping, where the climber and the rope are both at the bottom of the wall. As the climber ascends the wall, he will attach the rope into quick draws that are preplaced on the wall. Lead climbing should only be done by intermediate to advanced climbers, and most gyms do not allow lead climbing unless the climber is onsighting at least 5.10 and has been certified to lead.

Leading is more dangerous than toproping, as there is a chance for the climber to fall a greater distance when lead climbing. During a lead climb, the climber clips into a quick draw, then climbs above that quick draw to the next.

Quick draws in the gym are typically 3 to 6 feet apart. The farther apart the quick draws, the farther the potential fall for the climber. If a climber falls before reaching the next quick draw, the fall will be double the distance from the quick draw, plus the stretch in the rope. In the drawing, you can see that the climber is 5 feet above the last quick draw. She will fall double the distance to the quick draw, plus the amount of rope that is out (5 feet + another 5 feet + stretch in rope).

As this lead climber falls, the rope stretches before she comes to a stop well below her top quick draw.

WHAT DO THE RATINGS MEAN?

At the base of climbs in a gym, there is usually a written number to represent the difficulty of the climb.

The ratings for climbs in gyms in the United States are usually based on the Yosemite Decimal System, although some gyms make up their own rating system. Such is the case at CATS in Boulder, Colorado, where Rob Candelaria uses the "Chili" system so as not to confuse the gym ratings with outdoor ratings.

The more typical Yosemite Decimal System is for toprope and lead climbs and starts with a "5" then a "." followed by another number. The "5" tells you that the climb should be done while roped up. (Based on "fourth" class, which is hiking, "fifth" class is climbing with ropes.) When you say the grade 5.10, you would pronounce it as "five ten." Below is the basic level of each number after the fifth-class rating for a gym setting. This scale is the same for outdoor climbing but may feel different on natural rock.

YOSEMITE DECIMAL SYSTEM (RATINGS)

- 5.4–5.6 (the typical start of the scale, considered recreational)

- 5.7–5.8 (beginner climbs)

- 5.9–5.10 (the start of the intermediate climbs, getting more difficult) A climber will probably need some technique to get to the top.

- 5.11 (intermediate climbs) More techniques come into play, such as backstepping, underclings, and weight shifts.

- 5.12 (advanced climbs) Getting into the higher numbers, letters are added to the end of the rating to specify just how difficult it is. If a climb has an "a" it is easier than "b." Letters go up to "d," which is almost as difficult as the next number grade up; for example, 5.12d is very similar to 5.13a.

- 5.13 (very advanced)

- 5.14–5.15 (extremely difficult, professional climbing level) There are several 5.14's, but only one or two possible 5.15's exist in the world.

Another rating system that must be mentioned is the Verm scale. John Sherman, major developer of one of the premier bouldering areas in the country—Hueco Tanks, near El Paso, Texas—is noted for having the modern-day bouldering rating system named after him. When he was developing Hueco, the system used for boulder problems didn't take into account the levels of problems once they were completed, thus the "V" system was christened. Only physical difficulty counts on the Verm scale, with the rating remaining the same whether the problem is toproped or bouldered. These ratings are a consensus from the opinions of boulderers, starting with V0 and (on this date) ending at V15. This scale applies whether bouldering outdoors or indoors.

WHAT IS A ROUTE?

A route is a series of specific holds used to get to the top of the wall. Routes are rated for difficulty, and if only the holds designated on the route are used, the climber has climbed that particular route. Roped routes in the United States are rated using the Yosemite Decimal System, while boulder problems are rated on the V scale.

WHY IS THERE COLORED TAPE ON THE WALL?

The colored tape at the edge of climbing holds designates different routes up the wall. By following only one color of tape to the top of the wall, the route will have a specific rating. Usually the rating of a particular climb will be marked at the bottom of the climb (on the starting hold tape), or there will be a map in the gym designating the ratings of each climb.

Just because one "blue route" is 5.9, however, does not indicate that every route with blue tape has the same rating. Route setters don't always know when they start taping a route if it will be 5.9 or 5.10, so it would be difficult to have all the same grade be the same color. Ratings usually cannot be determined until after the route has been climbed, sometimes by more than one person.

WHY ARE THE WALLS AT DIFFERENT ANGLES?

The walls in a climbing gym are different angles—slabby, overhanging, vertical—to offer more terrain for the climbers. A slab climb is similar to climbing a ladder that is leaning against a wall. An overhanging wall is like climbing on the underside of a ladder and can have various degrees of angles. If a gym is all vertical, climbers can get bored of always climbing the same type of routes for example, crimpy or slopey. If a gym is all overhanging, climbers won't improve on slabby terrain.

A good gym has various terrain so that climbers can have enough variety to work all aspects of climbing techniques. Just because there is an overhang, though, doesn't mean that all the routes are difficult. Usually route setters try to put a range of ratings up on all surfaces of the gym so that beginners and professionals can climb different route styles.

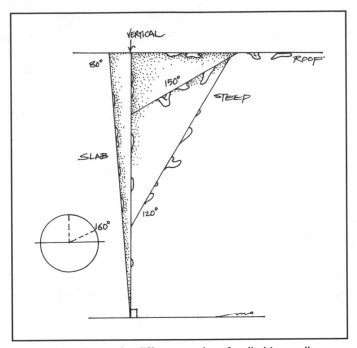

This drawing shows the different angles of a climbing wall.

WHY ARE THE HOLDS DIFFERENT COLORS?

Holds on the wall can be different colors based on what each manufacturer produces. Some hold companies only have blue holds, whereas most have a variety of colors and textures to their holds.

It is important for gyms to have a variety of manufacturers' holds in their gym so that their clientele is able to climb on a good mixture of holds. If a gym buys holds from only one manufacturer, the climbers in that gym will not know what other holds are like and may struggle when climbing in other gyms.

Some gyms use the colors of the holds to designate individual routes, but it can be difficult to distinguish among them when climbing on the wall. Blue and green holds can look alike from above. This method of route setting saves the gym from using tape on the wall surface.

Climbers competing in other gyms must be familiar with as many holds as possible so that they know what to expect when reaching for a hold.

WHAT ABOUT CLIMBING OUTSIDE?

Climbing outside can be extremely safe, as long as students have the proper instruction and supervision. Many people think they can learn to climb in a gym and then just go outside and climb, but there are many differences.

The major distinction between climbing in a gym and climbing outside is that the topropes are not set up for you outside. In order to set up topropes outside, you must know how to place gear and equalize anchors, know the rock (some is more stable than others), know the area and which climbs are the proper rating for your level of climbing, and know proper etiquette. Before climbing outside alone, be sure to get proper instruction.

Even leading a sport climb outside is different from leading in the gym. Outdoors the draws are not prehung, bolts can be farther apart, routes must be cleaned (draws removed), and the anchor must be changed over for lowering. All of these issues can make climbing outdoors far more challenging than climbing in a gym, where everything is basically set up for the climber.

Climbing outdoors is so much fun that your students will probably want to do it. Chapter 17, Let's Go Climbing!, is a good introduction to climbing outdoors, but make sure you also get professional instruction before climbing or coaching on natural rock.

HOW CAN I TELL IF A GYM IS SAFE?

Here are some signs that the gym is safe:

- A safe gym has proper supervision of the climbing area at all times.

- Employees are walking around periodically, checking to make sure things are running safely.

- A log book is used by gym employees to ensure proper maintenance of ropes and other equipment.

- Periodic changes and upgrades to the gym show that the owner/manager is interested in making improvements for the members and not just in business to make money. Upgrades can be as simple as new holds and ropes or as complex as a new feature on a wall.

- Holds are cleaned when they are removed from the wall before they are put back up. This shows that gym personnel are inspecting the holds and maintaining the equipment.

- New routes are put up periodically and old routes taken down.

- The gym is clean, although there will always be dust due to chalk.

- There is adequate padding under all climbing surfaces—especially bouldering areas—and the climbing areas are free of obstacles such as ladders and chairs.

- Employees are knowledgeable about climbing, but that doesn't necessarily mean they know everything. Check around with different sources—books, other employees, climbers—for answers to important questions.

- While they are on the clock, employees are more concerned about your needs than their own personal climbing time. Most gym employees are very interested in how you or your students are improving and love to talk about climbing.

- When you're checking in at the front desk, gym employees make sure that you have signed waivers and have the authority to be there.

- The first time you climb in a gym, you are always checked for belay skills and the proper ability to tie in to a rope. If you are a lead climber, you must pass a lead test before climbing.

- Questions are immediately answered by the staff. If you still have a question about a safety or climbing issue after speaking with an employee, speak with a manager.

- Even new employees of the gym have climbing knowledge. It is impossible to supervise a climbing gym safely without knowing basic climbing safety rules.

Coaching

WHAT QUALIFICATIONS ARE NECESSARY FOR COACHING CLIMBING?

Although an extensive climbing background is not necessary to coach climbing, a slight knowledge of climbing is. Even if this knowledge stops after the basics, anyone with the ability to teach should be able to coach climbing.

A coach is someone who can help another person improve his performance, even if that person is a better climber than she is. This fact alone makes it possible for a nonclimber to coach climbing. If a nonclimber can see what a climber is doing wrong, and express it in a way to help the climber improve, he can teach climbing.

During my years of directing the U.S. Climbing Team Junior Pro Camps, I found that some of the top climbers in the country, adult members of the U.S. Climbing Team, were unable to coach successfully. They could not see what a student needed to do to improve. Sometimes they could not even see what they personally needed to work on. Remember, some people are born teachers; others are not.

On the other hand, sometimes a really good climber may not be able to tell someone what she is doing incorrectly, but that good climber may be able to demonstrate techniques well. This can be good for a visually oriented student—one who learns from seeing rather than listening to instruction.

As the coach, you can find your strengths and play off of them. If you are unable to demonstrate techniques but know what is right and what is wrong, enlist the help of a good climber for the times when visualization is needed.

Don't forget to reward your students for working hard for you! You can do this through the awards that come with climbing competitions, or just give your students some free climbing time during their season.

Let the parents of your student know what your credentials are so that they can make an informed decision whether to hire you as a coach. Be honest if you are new at coaching the sport, and charge accordingly.

HOW MANY KIDS CAN I COACH AT ONE TIME?

This falls somewhat under safety aspects, depending on the experience of the climbers you are coaching. Think of how many beginning climbers you can safely watch on the wall, and decide for yourself what your maximum number of students should be. Even if your students are more advanced, and there is absolutely no question as to their safety while belaying, determine how many students you can instruct and effectively give your attention to at one time.

Personally, when I give my "Beyond the Basics" clinics across the United States, I find that my ideal number of students is six. These clinics are four hours long, so there is plenty of time for me to get to know the students and their climbing needs. Sometimes gyms sign up more than my maximum, and it completely changes the dynamics of the group for me. With six climbers, I can have three climbing and three belaying at any given time, and I am able to give the three climbers on the wall very individual instruction.

When I am hired to work with teams at different climbing gyms on a single clinic basis, most gyms tend to overbook my session. During a two-hour clinic, if I have ten kids, I feel that all I can do is give them instructions and that's about it. There is no time to watch each one and get familiar with his individual climbing style. Usually I end up working with only a couple of the team members, and the others fall through the cracks.

For me, the smaller the group, the better. It is my personal feeling that when I am hired to coach, I need to be "coaching"—offering constant advice while a student is on the wall, watching the climbers' movements, helping each climber with individual moves, etc. Climbing is very technical, and it is impossible to watch yourself do it unless you are videotaped. For a student, the coach is an extra set of eyes, there to help when techniques need improvement.

HOW DO I COACH WHEN I KNOW NOTHING?

Knowing nothing about climbing does not mean that you can't coach. This book is an excellent place to start—the more you know, the better you will be able to coach. There are numerous videos you can watch and books you can read. You can talk to other coaches or climbers and get ideas and suggestions.

If you honestly know absolutely nothing about climbing, you must start off with an introductory lesson at a gym. This lesson will go over tying into a rope and belaying and will give you a safety base from which to start teaching. Typically that is where an introductory lesson ends. You can also take a basic climbing technique class, which is offered at most gyms. If you can climb—even a little—it will give you a much better appreciation of what you are asking your student to do.

One thing you will learn once you start hanging out in a gym is that people who climb love the sport. Chances are you will develop that same enjoyment, and so will your students. It's addicting, so beware!

WHAT DO I DO WHEN THE KIDS GET OUT OF CONTROL?

Whenever you get a group of kids together, there will be a few that don't conform. In a climbing gym, however, it is vitally important that everyone act safely.

Safely means that kids cannot be running around out of control in the gym. For one thing, it is distracting; secondly, it can be dangerous. Think about a kid bumping into a belayer. What if the belayer has to reach out to balance himself and takes his brake hand off the rope? This endangers the climber, as she is essentially off belay when the belayer's brake hand is removed from the rope.

There are numerous ways to make sure your group is under control. The best way is to limit the number of students you coach to six. The smaller the group, the easier they will be to manage. For those kids who do not want to take the responsibility of belaying and acting properly, you will have to come up with rewards and punishments. One idea is to always have "free" climbing at the end of practice, letting the kids climb whatever routes they would like. If a student is out of control during practice, you can change that "free" climbing into an exercise of some sort and have the student work on his least favorite move or technique. Another idea is always to have a game at the end of practice. If one student is misbehaving, take away the game for the entire group. This makes kids responsible not only for their own actions but also for the entire team. Peer pressure will help keep everyone under control.

HOW MANY TIMES SHOULD MY KIDS CLIMB THE SAME ROUTE?

Quite often a climber may get on the same route over and over again. This is beneficial for setting moves into the muscle memory (engrams) but it can get boring. Sometimes a climber may just enjoy a route and want to keep climbing it, which is fine. Make sure that if you have a climber doing the same route multiple times, she is also getting on routes that she is not as good at or routes that are a different style. The more types of routes a climber attempts, the better rounded her climbing style will be.

HOW OFTEN SHOULD MY KIDS TRY NEW ROUTES?

No matter what level of climber you are working with, you do not want her to get bored climbing the same route over and over again. Be sure to have a variety of routes available for your student to climb.

Sometimes it is necessary for a climber to climb the same route multiple times—working endurance is a good example. If you are repeating the same route for an exercise, understand that the moves will become ingrained in the muscle memory (engrams) of the student and that the route grade will essentially be lowered as the climber becomes accustomed to the moves on that route. When you watch a climber on something she has climbed before, the movement will look more fluid and controlled than on something she is climbing for the first time. This is a prime example of muscle memory.

Variety is important to any training program. If you do not have a lot of routes in all the grade levels at your gym, talk with the gym owner/manager and make sure a plan is in place for replacing routes after they have been up awhile—anything longer than two months is too long.

HOW OFTEN SHOULD MY KIDS CLIMB DURING A WEEK?

Your students should expect to climb at least two times a week to maintain their climbing level. Three times a week and the climber will see improvements; four times a week and the advancement rate will be phenomenal—especially for a new/beginning climber.

Unfortunately, if a climber is only able to climb one to two times a week, each climbing session will be focused on relearning moves. Muscles will not be accustomed to the movement and will not develop the endurance necessary for harder routes.

HOW LONG SHOULD A CLIMBER BE IN THE GYM?

Ideally, the time spent climbing should be longer than two hours—optimally, four—but it's better to judge that time by routes completed rather than by a clock. When you are dealing with young kids, there are numerous time restraints, such as school, homework, other activities, and family time. Fortunately, young climbers have natural flexibility and movement without having to spend as much time on the wall as older climbers, and two hours per session is sufficient. If you have a climber who is interested in being the best in the country, however, she will need to climb four days a week, three to four hours per session. My baseline in the gym is to climb around twelve routes in a session.

HOW DO I COMMUNICATE WITH A CLIMBER 20 FEET ABOVE ME?

One of the most difficult aspects of coaching can be the distance between the climber and the coach. If you are coaching in a 40-foot-high gym and the gym is open to the public, the noise level can be quite high. There are a few ways to deal with this situation:

- A laser pointer can be an extremely useful tool for a coach, especially when you are telling your climber which hold to grab or step on. This eliminates saying "that flat green hold" and having the climber search frantically for it. Instead you can just point. Remember, though, laser pointers are not permitted at most climbing competitions. This is a tool to be used during practice.

- Give a detailed lesson on the ground, using the first couple of holds as examples. Have the climber do the exercise for a couple of moves—basically bouldering, without a belay—and then come down. Make sure the concept of the exercise is grasped before he ties in so that you don't have to keep explaining as he is climbing. Stop him close to the ground if he is doing something improperly, and make sure it is done correctly before he continues climbing to the top.

- Only communicate until the climber is halfway up the wall. Before that point, give detailed corrections to the climber so that there are no more mistakes after the halfway point. Once the climber has the concept completely engrained, the second half of the climb is just a matter of reinforcing the proper engrams (muscle memory) in the body by doing the moves correctly.

AT WHAT AGE SHOULD A CHILD BEGIN COMPETING?

The USCCA (formerly the JCCA) has a category for eleven years and younger, so any age climber can compete. For the most part, when a gym hosts a regional USCCA competition, it is relatively informal and just plain fun for the climbers. While the USCCA regional competitions are relatively informal, the national-level competitions are onsight format and become more structured and isolate climbers. During onsight competitions, climbers are held in a warm-up area until it is their turn to climb, so they climb the route without having seen anyone else on it. Because climbers are not allowed to talk with one another about the routes before climbing them, there is a lot less socializing and more stress at onsight competitions. For more advanced climbers, onsight competitions are a great opportunity to improve and develop other facets of climbing, such as concentration, onsight skills, and mental preparation. For younger climbers, stick with the fun, local competitions or USCCA events.

HOW MANY COMPETITIONS ARE REASONABLE DURING A MONTH?

The USCCA competitions can be frequent if you have students participating in the entire series. Sometimes these competitions are twice a month, which is a lot, especially if you live in a large region. When you have frequent competitions, it can sometimes feel as though all you are doing is preparing for the next competition. As long as it is still fun for the climber, compete in as many as the climber wants to, but if it becomes a chore go back to climbing for fun and skip the comps.

A competition per month is a reasonable number, and it allows climbers to compare themselves with others and see their improvement based on that comparison.

HOW FAST WILL MY STUDENT IMPROVE?

One nice thing about coaching young climbers is that you will be able to see improvement in their climbing skills from week to week—if they are climbing twice a week. Young climbers do not need as much recovery time as adults and usually don't experience such overuse injuries as tendonitis.

I have seen complete beginners climbing 5.11 within a few months and other young climbers struggle to climb 5.10 after a couple of years. The main factor in this improvement is the time the climbers devote to climbing, as well as their natural ability to climb.

Muscle mass does not factor into climbing as much as you might imagine. A climber who uses pure strength to muscle up climbs will not learn technique or improve as quickly as a climber who learns how to climb using technique.

When I started climbing, 5.11 was considered extremely difficult; only a few climbs rated higher than that. For me—and many other climbers of my generation—that grade became a significant mental barrier. Today, young climbers see average people climbing 5.12, so that seems a natural grade to strive for. If 5.12 is not perceived as difficult for a young climber, she will achieve that grade a lot faster than someone who sees it as a barrier.

Each climber will advance through the grades at a different pace, and climbers should not be compared with one another. One climber may have great endurance and be able to climb 5.11's all day long but never pull through a 5.12; whereas another student may be able to climb 5.12 easily and not be able to climb two 5.11's back to back. Have your students set achievable goals—short and long term—and do everything in your power to help them accomplish those goals.

Safety

HOW OLD SHOULD A CHILD BE BEFORE BELAYING?

Each gym will have a definitive policy about when a child can belay. In most gyms around the country, kids under twelve are not allowed to belay, but in some gyms the age is even higher. This age is based on several things, the first of which is attention span. If a child cannot be counted on to concentrate on belaying but instead watches other climbers and talks, then he is not ready for the responsibility of belaying.

The other major factor for belaying is the size of the belayer versus the size of the climber. A belayer must be large enough to catch a climber in the event of a fall. Catching a climber does not just mean catching the weight of a climber, it also takes into account the force of the fall, which can be substantial based on the distance of the fall. I would question any gym's policy if they allow kids younger than twelve to belay. The responsibility for the safety of another human being should not be placed on young children.

If you are coaching children younger than twelve, you may need to enlist another climber or a parent to belay during your coaching sessions.

With smaller climbers, the belayer may have to force-feed the rope through the belay device during the lowering process. With some belay devices, a lighter weight climber doesn't have enough weight on the rope to be lowered down with just the friction of the rope running through the device, so the rope will have to be fed through. During this process, it is imperative that the belayer always keeps the brake hand on the rope.

SHOULD MY STUDENTS WEAR HELMETS?

Helmets are a personal preference in gyms, even though wearing a helmet sounds like a safety issue. In a climbing gym, there is very little risk of rocks falling from above, which is probably the number-one injury in outdoor climbing. Indoors, the biggest factor for injury would be falling upside down and hitting the head on the wall. A helmet would prevent serious injury from this type of fall, but the risk for this type of injury is low.

If a helmet is worn in a gym, make sure it fits snuggly and does not slide back on the head exposing the forehead.

For students climbing outdoors, wearing a helmet is mandatory.

SHOULD PARENTS LEAVE THEIR CHILD ALONE TO CLIMB IN THE GYM?

If the child is a complete beginner, I would not leave him alone, even with a team. I have heard of teams that do not allow parents to watch or take part in practice, which I question from a safety standpoint. As a parent, I would like to know that the safety practices are in place before leaving my child alone in a training session.

If a child is climbing in an after-school program and only adults are belaying, then it would be reasonable to leave a child alone in a climbing gym. Once a child has learned to belay and tie in properly, and has a sense of safety, she could be left alone—with some adult supervision in the gym—to climb with a partner. I would also set an age limit or find out if the gym has one already in place.

One thing that must be stressed to a child is not to climb with strangers, unless the gym employees have personal knowledge of the other person's climbing experience. I have seen professional climbers dropped—to the ground—at the gym and outside when they have partnered with a stranger. It is always better to be safe than sorry.

IS CLIMBING DANGEROUS?

I never think of climbing in a gym as dangerous, as long as the proper protocol is followed. For liability reasons alone, most gyms are safe and make sure their members are safety-conscious. Remember, though, that most climbing accidents are caused by human error. Belaying and tying in are basic safety elements. Proper communication must be used at all times. When climbing outside, a helmet and appropriate instruction are mandatory (see Chapter 2 for basic climbing skills). As long as safety regulations are followed, it is rare to have a climbing accident.

Setting Problems and Routes

One of the biggest issues when training climbers is making sure the routes or boulder problems that are being used are appropriate for the activities you design for your students. Hopefully the gym you coach at has quality route setters and you can work directly with them for your needs. If you find yourself using a private/home gym or a commercial facility that cannot accommodate your needs, you may be responsible for setting many of your own problems. There are also times when you need a specific problem that may not be readily available to work on a specific technique.

In this section and throughout the book, you will notice the terms *route* and *problem* are used interchangeably. A route is basically a climb that goes from the bottom of the wall to the top and must be climbed with a rope—either lead or toprope. In bouldering, the term *problem* is more appropriate because it refers to a shorter version of a route with far fewer moves, most of which will be difficult for the climber. When setting a route, remember that it should be relatively long, with twenty or more moves. A boulder problem can be much shorter with as few as one move to target a specific technique. If you are using a bouldering wall for most of your practice, you can set routes that are low to the ground. Instead of going up, the route traverses, so a rope is not needed. Routes on a bouldering wall are basically just long boulder problems.

A quality route is recognized by movements that are fun and natural, while still being challenging. Setting routes is a craft that can take years to develop. However, you may not have the time or desire to learn the art of route setting.

One of the basic mistakes made by beginning route setters is increasing a problem's difficulty by just extending the distance of the holds. This makes a problem more challenging for a shorter climber but probably won't change the difficulty if the climber can still reach the hold. Another common mistake is trying to make the problem more interesting by using holds in a way that they were not intended to be used.

The best way to make a problem more difficult is to change the placement of the feet or make the holds smaller—but don't make the mistake of using footholds as handholds. By changing the placement of the feet, you can change the entire body position of the climber, therefore making the move different or more difficult. If you have quality moves on a problem that are too easy for your student, instead of setting a new problem, just change out the holds to make it more challenging.

Use some variety when setting problems—try to not just use holds with the edge on top. Move the holds around so that you get some side pulls, gastons, and underclings. Mix up the footholds so that you have some small edges and slopers.

My favorite way to set boulder problems is to use holds that are already on the wall and tape problems without even getting out a wrench. With this method, the climber can try the moves and then move the tape to a different hold if the movement doesn't work.

If you actually have to screw holds onto the T-nuts on the wall, the challenge of setting routes will be more labor intensive. When putting up a route from scratch, you need to think about how both a short and a tall climber would do on the same move. You will have to put footholds where they will work for different types of climbers. The handholds will have to be within reach for all climbers, but not so close together that they are not challenging.

Whether you are setting problems with holds already on the wall or putting them up yourself, one of the route setting basics is to make sure the movement feels good. Have you ever climbed a problem and felt as though each move was awkward? Movement should feel smooth and comfortable, but that does not mean a climber shouldn't have to grunt through a move every now and then. Each individual move should be close to the same difficulty level. The problem shouldn't go from a cakewalk to a complete shutdown. Also, moves shouldn't be impossible; they should be attainable with some work.

Talk to local route setters for advice. Set some problems, and have climbers get on them and give you feedback. Don't take the comments personally; it takes a lot of time to develop a feel for setting problems. If you set a problem that isn't good, change it! The more you set, the easier it will get.

Chapter 2: **From the Ground Up**

If you are coaching a kid who has never climbed before, a series of steps must be mastered before the serious coaching can begin. Start with these basics; when they are mastered, you can then develop your program.

One of the most important things for a beginning climber is to have fun. If possible, start all new climbers with something easy so that they can get to the top of the wall and feel successful right from the beginning. The best thing that can happen is that the student will get hooked and want to come back for more. The worst thing that can happen is that the child decides climbing is not for her based on an unsuccessful first climb.

When I became a professional climber, my dad was stunned! He reminded me of the first time he and I had ever climbed (at a scout camp in New Mexico) and how I had cried all the way down as I was rappelling. After climbing for twenty more years, obviously I have overcome my fears. Even if a person doesn't take to the sport immediately, make sure you provide encouragement—and a second chance.

Starting at the very beginning, anyone interested in taking up climbing should go through a basic climbing lesson—offered at all climbing gyms. If you are an experienced climber, you can give this instruction to your students; if you are not, make sure they get a professional lesson. This lesson will include putting on a harness, tying into the rope, helmet pointers, belaying, and basic climbing instruction. These five elements are detailed here so that you know what to expect from a basic climbing lesson.

Harness

1. Depending on the size of the child, there are numerous types of harnesses available. Harness rental is typically included in the first lesson given at the gym. If a student decides she really enjoys the sport, a harness can be purchased at any major outdoor sport store, such as Eastern Mountain Sports, REI, Galyans, and other local dealers, including most climbing gyms.

2. A climbing harness should fit snugly around the legs and have a close-fitting waist belt. Sometimes the leg belts can be adjusted for a tighter fit.

3. A young climber who is too slender in the hip area may be given a "body harness" to use. This type of harness goes around the shoulders as well as the legs so that the climber is safe in the event of hanging upside down. A small climber could easily fall out of a traditional harness if he has no extruding hip bones to hold it in place.

4. Because there are so many styles, when fitting a harness, remember that it should be snug around the legs and waist; it will loosen slightly during climbing as it adjusts to the body.

5. The first thing you need to inspect when using a rental harness is abnormal or excessive wear. Make sure there are no thin spots in the webbing—especially where the rope ties in. If there are buckles that unhook, make sure they have been put together properly and that they double back. Also check that the webbing lies flat without twists.

6. Any exposed buckles should be "doubled back" so that the webbing goes all the way through the buckle (like a belt) and then returns through the buckle in the opposite direction (see illustration at right).

7. Have the harness checked by a gym employee if there is any doubt about the fit or reliability of the harness.

All Tied Up

1. Tying into the rope is something every climber—and belayer—must master before climbing. There are two knots used to tie the rope into the harness: the retraced figure-8 and the bowline. The figure-8 is standard; however, the bowline is sometimes used by larger climbers, because it is easier to untie if it gets tightened down by falls. Groups climbing together should use the same knot so that it can be checked properly.

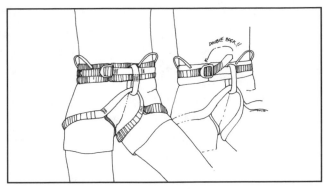

A properly fitting harness should be snug around the legs and waist, with the waist belt webbing doubled back through the buckle to prevent it from coming undone.

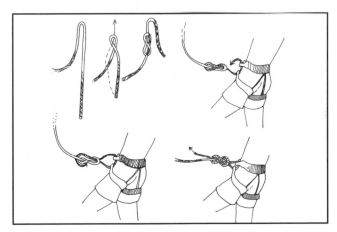

Be sure to get proper knot-tying instruction before tying in with a figure-8.

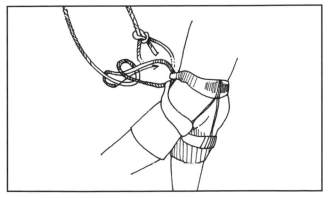

Not as popular as the figure-8 knot for tying into the rope, the bowline is also used.

2. One important safety aspect to note is that each person is ultimately responsible for tying her own knots and checking to make sure her partner is tied in properly. This gives a backup for each person—one person ties the knot, the other double-checks it.

3. When tying into a toprope, the climber ties in at the opposite end of the rope—hanging closer to the wall—than the belayer. The climber ties a figure-8 knot in the rope, leaving about 2 feet of extra rope, and then puts the short end of the rope through the harness. (Some harnesses have a "belay loop," but it should not be used to tie in to the rope.) The rope should go through the leg loops where they are connected together and then up through the waist belt. Now the figure-8 knot can be "retraced."

4. Each climber must get proper instruction on how to tie into the rope before climbing. If in doubt, have a gym employee check the knot before climbing. There is no excuse for climbing without tying in properly. A climbing gym would rather check the knot each time than have an accident occur.

Brain Bucket

1. When signing waivers at the climbing gym, one of the first decisions to make is whether to sign the helmet waiver. By signing the waiver, the climber is saying that he will not wear a helmet. Most accidents in which a helmet would prevent injury occur due to falling rock. The main dangers in a gym are from falling too far and hitting the head or from a hold being dropped from above by a route setter. A helmet would help in either of these instances.

2. If a helmet is worn, make sure it fits properly and does not wiggle around. A helmet that is worn too far back on the head will not prevent an injury to the forehead. If it is too far forward, it will not prevent an injury to the back of the neck.

3. Make sure any helmet used for climbing is approved by the UIAA (Union Internationale des Associations D'Alpinisme) or the International Mountaineering and Climbing Federation.

On Belay

1. One of the most serious jobs in climbing is being responsible for another person's safety. That is the main job of the belayer. The belayer's job can be tedious because she is standing on the ground and pulling up the rope as the climber has all the fun going up the wall. It is vitally important that the belayer pay attention to the climber at all times. The belayer is the only person, besides a coach, who should be conversing with the climber—and *only* the climber! There should be no talking with other people on the ground—or watching any climber except the one at the other end of the belayer's rope.

2. At what age should a young climber be allowed to belay? Some gyms have strict age regulations, with most gyms recommending twelve years or older. In my opinion, anyone allowed to belay must be mature enough to take another person's life in his hands and understand the implications of how important the belaying job is. The belayer must be able to concentrate completely on the task at hand.

3. Another consideration for belaying is the size of the climber versus the size of the belayer. If the climber is significantly larger than the belayer, the belayer must be tied down—anchored—to the ground, or a larger belayer should be used. If a belayer is even fifteen pounds lighter than the climber, I would recommend clipping that belayer into an anchor. More force than just the fifteen-pound weight difference comes into play when a person falls, and the belayer must be prepared for that.

4. The belayer is also responsible for understanding how to use the belay device she is using and for locking the carabiner onto her harness before belaying. For example, the belay device can be attached to the harness backward, with the rope feeding through to the left if the belayer is right-handed. This must be checked before the climber leaves the ground, because it changes the brake hand for the belayer. A more experienced belayer should be comfortable belaying with either hand, but a beginning belayer might not have this ability.

5. The belayer must be proficient—beyond any fault—in the following activities before being allowed to belay without supervision:

• Make sure the belayer and climber are tied into the same rope.

• The belay device must be attached to the harness properly, with the rope feeding out the proper direction for brake purposes.

• Make sure the climber will go in-line vertically to where the rope is anchored.

Belaying is an exact science. The belayer first pulls the rope up, taking up the slack, then the "brake" hand (in this case, right) slides down the rope—never letting go. The belayer can now "lock off" the rope so that it will not slide through the belay device.

- Take up the slack in the rope as the climber ascends on the wall.

- Lock off the climber if the climber is "resting" on the rope.

- Lower the climber slowly and in control when the climber is ready to come down off the climb.

- Never take the brake hand off the rope.

- Communicate with the climber at all times. If the climber is not comfortable, the belayer should be prepared to either take up any additional slack or lower the climber to the ground.

Ropes

1. At this point, I am assuming that you are coaching climbers inside a climbing gym. (Outdoor climbing will be addressed in Chapter 17, Let's Go Climbing!) In a climbing gym, the ropes are already attached to the upper part of the climbing wall and have been safety tested.

2. Ropes can be attached to the upper part of a climbing wall in a number of ways. Some may go through two carabiners, others may be wrapped around a bar, and still others may go through "cold shuts," which are rounded metal brackets. All of these methods are safe, as long as there are two points of contact between the rope and the wall. (Although using the rope wrapped around the bar does not have two points of contact with the actual wall, the bar is typically welded into two metal braces, making it one of the safest methods available.)

3. The ropes used in climbing gyms for toprope climbing are either "gym ropes" or static lines. Both of these types of rope give very little stretch if a climber falls, making the climber feel more secure when on the wall. Dynamic ropes are usually used for lead climbing, but they are sometimes put on a toprope wall. Dynamic ropes will "give" a little if the climber puts weight on the rope, which can feel as though the belayer has given out slack, when in fact it is just the rope stretching.

4. Even though ropes are the gym's responsibility, if at any point you feel that a rope is too thin or the sheath is worn, immediately bring it to the attention of the gym manager. Never climb on a rope that you are not comfortable with.

Communication

1. Now that the climber is tied into the rope using a retraced figure-8 knot (or bowline) and the belayer has attached himself to the other end of the rope with his belay device and locking carabiner, it is almost time for the fun to begin.

2. Before climbing, the climber and belayer must communicate so that the climber knows she has the undivided attention of her belayer. The commands start with the climber and end with the belayer as follows:

   Climber: *"On belay?"* The climber is tied into the rope and should now check to make sure the belay device is on the proper end of the rope and attached correctly to the belayer's harness. If the gym requires belayers to be anchored to the ground, this should also be double-checked.

   Belayer: *"Your belay is on."* The belayer checks to make sure the climber's knot is tied properly into the harness and that the harness is on correctly—all webbing is doubled back. The belayer also double-checks the belay device on his own harness and makes sure his carabiner is locked, with the rope going through correctly.

Climber: *"Climbing."* The climber now steps up to the wall so that the belayer can take up any extra slack in the rope, but she does not start climbing until the belayer has responded.

Belayer: *"Climb on."* The belayer now has all the slack out of the rope and is prepared to take up the rope as the climber begins to climb. The belayer should never respond until he is ready to give his full attention to the climber.

3. Once the climber has started climbing, a few other commands can be used between the climber and belayer. These commands are pretty standard and should be easily understood, even with someone you have never climbed with before. Any communication between the climber and belayer must be done in single words whenever possible. Most accidents happen when communication is misunderstood—mainly outdoors, where wind and distance can make communication difficult, but it can also happen in a climbing gym when there is a lot of noise.

Climber: *"Slack!"* The climber is asking the belayer to let out a little bit of rope. Chances are the rope is too tight and the climber is unable to move. This term is also used during lead climbing when the climber needs extra rope for clipping a quick draw.

Climber: *"Tension!"* The climber is asking the belayer to take up the rope. Sometimes the climber uses this command if it is a difficult move and she wants the reassurance of feeling the pressure of the rope.

Climber: *"Take."* The climber is asking the belayer to take up the slack in the rope, usually so that she can rest or has completed the climb and is ready to be lowered. At this point the belayer should take up all the slack and lock off the rope in the belay device.

Climber: *"Falling!"* This one is self-explanatory. Upon hearing this from a toproped climber, the belayer should make sure there is no slack in the rope and lock off the rope in the belay device.

Climber: *"Clipping."* The lead climber is ready to clip the rope into a quick draw and needs extra rope from the belayer. Some climbers expect the belayer to know when they need rope and may never ask for it. Other climbers may just tug on the rope until the belayer gives them the slack they need.

Climber: *"Down."* This means the climber is ready to be lowered to the ground. Another term used is *"Dirt me."*

Climber: *"Okay,"* *"Ready,"* or *"Take."* This means the climber is at the top of the climb and ready to come down. The belayer would respond with *"Gotcha!"* to let the climber know he is starting to lower her.

Belayer: *"Stop."* If the belayer is having trouble feeding out or taking up rope, he may need the climber to stop climbing while the problem is corrected.

Climbing in the Gym

1. Once the commands have been given, it is finally time for the climber to get off the ground. The first step should be a small one as the climber raises one foot off the floor and places it gently on a foothold. Now the hands can find holds, and the climber uses his leg to push off the ground to place his other foot on the wall.

2. One of the best things about kids is their natural ability to climb without thinking about anything except getting to the top of the wall. Let them go, but use the advice below to coach beginning climbers.

• Always use three points of contact. At all times, the climber should have either two feet and one hand or one foot and two hands on the wall. Only one hand and only one foot should be moved at a time—but not simultaneously. A climber who is moving a hand and a foot at the same time can lose his balance.

• Try not to pull with the arms. Use the legs to push up the wall.

• Kids are natural climbers and tend not to have a fear of heights. They are used to climbing on monkey bars and other playground equipment, much of which simulates climbing. Encourage young climbers to use momentum to get to the top of the wall. Young climbers are usually small, and they may see that as a disadvantage. In fact, using a little momentum, a small climber has the power to swing to moves that may seem out of reach.

- The climber should trust his belayer and relax during the climb. Some climbers tend to overgrip the holds, which will cause their forearms to tire quickly. Breathing and relaxing the arms are good ways to prevent this sort of tension.

- Above everything else—except safety—kids should be encouraged to have fun while climbing.

- If the climber is following a route (usually taped with colored duct tape), she should only use the holds designated for that route. Using holds with other colors of tape is considered going "off route" by some climbers and "cheating" by others.

Getting Down on Toprope

1. One of the scariest parts of climbing can be coming down. When a climber is ascending the wall, the rope and equipment are not helping the climber advance but are there for protection in case the climber slips and falls. When the climber gets to the top of the wall, she must now rely on the belayer and equipment to lower her to the ground.

2. Once the climber reaches the top of the wall, she should communicate to the belayer that she is ready to come down. This can be done verbally, but there is really no set command. Most climbers just say "Take," "Ready," or "Okay." The belayer now takes up all the slack in the rope.

3. Once the slack is taken out of the system, the climber lets go of the holds and leans back on the rope. Her feet should be directly in front of her body and even with her waist.

4. As the belayer begins to lower the climber, the climber should walk backward down the wall, keeping pace with the amount of rope the belayer is letting out. The climber does not have any control over the speed at which she is being lowered, except to say "Slower" or "Faster."

5. While the belayer controls the speed of the descent, he should be aware that lowering too quickly damages the ropes, anchors, and belay devices because speed equals heat. The belayer must be able to control the rope. If it is going too fast through the belay device, it can get out of control quickly. It is difficult to stop a rope that is going through a belay device out of control. I know many belayers who have gotten rope burn while trying to stop a climber from

falling to the ground because either the belay device was threaded incorrectly or they let the rope go too quickly.

6. There is usually no need for the belayer to stop the climber during the lowering process unless the rope is kinked. The rope should move smoothly through the belay device so that the climber doesn't have a jerky ride to the ground.

7. As the climber is lowered, she should keep her feet about shoulder width apart. If the feet are too close together, the body can sway to one side and hit the wall.

8. If the feet are too low on the wall as the climber is being lowered, it is easy for the feet to slip and the body to hit the wall.

9. Many climbers want to "bounce" down the wall, pushing off and getting a distance from the wall before touching in with the feet. This method of lowering down the wall is hard on the equipment (ropes and anchors). The proper method of lowering off the wall is simply to walk down backward.

10. The angle of the wall changes the ease of lowering off a climb. If the wall is a slab (leaning like a ladder against a building), the climber will walk backward

The proper position when lowering off a climb—feet against the wall at about hip level, weight on the rope, and hands on the knot. Photo: Stewart Green

but may have trouble keeping her feet at hip level. If the wall is vertical (straight up and down), it will be easy for the climber to walk backward down the wall. When the wall begins to overhang (as in the underside of a roof), the climber may not be touching the wall at all and just be lowered into space by the rope.

The End

Once the climber has reached the ground, she will typically untie from the rope and switch places with the belayer, allowing the belayer to climb and the climber to belay. The climber should say "Off belay," to indicate that she is safely on the ground. The belayer responds with "Your belay is off," telling the climber that he is no longer responsible for the climber's safety.

Chapter 3:
Hit the Ground Running—
the Starting Box

At some competitions, the starting hold for a route is found inside a taped box. This hold is the start of the route, and any climber climbing the route must start with both hands inside the box. This gives all climbers equal advantage by starting on the same hold, whether the climber is short or tall, forcing all competitors to perform the same opening move on the route. A climber who does not follow the rules and has only one hand in the designated box is immediately disqualified from the competition.

By using this concept and starting your student in the "starting box," you are explaining the rules and outlining what is expected. Starting on an even playing field is important, not just for your climbers but also for you.

Your Starting Box

Where do you start coaching? In order to determine your students' abilities, you will first need to evaluate each student's climbing skills (see Chapter 4). Once you know what needs to be worked on, you can develop a plan for each individual student. Develop your session schedule around what your student needs. The initial starting box should include exercises that work any techniques that are lacking. The weaknesses you originally identified through the climbing evaluation will need to be updated as the climber improves each technique.

If a student lacks rudimentary climbing skills, such as precise footwork or backstepping techniques, you will probably need to start that climber on basic technique-oriented sessions for about a month.

Students who already have basic climbing skills will need to show you that they have mastered them. This is the time to correct any bad habits the climber has developed while climbing without a coach. Bad habits include lack of resting, imprecise footwork, and not breathing. Once bad habits are corrected—probably in just a couple of practices—you will need to identify any other weaknesses and work on those, including endurance, power, power-endurance, and clipping.

There will *always* be something that each of your climbers will need to work on. Even the top climbers in the world have areas that can be improved, however minute those areas might be. No climber has perfect form, and any area of imperfection becomes a weakness. Make sure your students understand that while they will never have everything down to perfection, they will be improving with every climbing session.

The Coach

"If you think your coach is tough, wait until you get a boss."

COMMITMENT

As the coach, you will need to make a huge time commitment that will probably extend beyond coaching at the gym. Take a good look at everything that is involved, and truly commit once you have decided to act as coach. There is nothing worse than a coach who does not show up, or quits in the middle of the season.

The time allotment for coaching will vary from student to student. Some students will meet with you only once a week; others will meet with you more frequently (see "The Schedule" later in this chapter). Whatever time commitment you believe it will take, plan on more. Believe me, you will be doing more than just coaching. My phone rings at all hours. My students call to tell me how they did in a competition or to share their excitement about an ascent. There are also numerous phone discussions with parents to work out travel arrangements or attitude adjustments. Coordinating efforts with other coaches, personal trainers, yoga instructors, etc., will also fall under your jurisdiction so that your climbers achieve the best all-around fitness level.

RESPONSIBILITY

When you pledge to be the coach, you are committing to more than just the time it takes to hang out in the gym while your students climb. You are responsible for coming up with activities, making sure they are stretching, determining if a student with an injury needs to sit out, and keeping the sessions exciting and fresh each and every week.

You will know if your coaching is successful if your students stick with it and are excited to be there each week. If your climbers come in asking, "What are we doing today?" you know they are anticipating the next thing you have invented to help them become better climbers. To be a good coach you will need all the resources you can get your hands on. This book is an excellent starting place, but there are several other books you can read to get more ideas (see the Resources section in the Appendix). *Climbing* and *Rock & Ice* magazines also have wonderful tips and pointers each month that you can incorporate into your coaching.

As the coach, you likely will be responsible for most of the following:

- Planning each practice/training session

- Performing evaluations on your climbers

- Teaching basic climbing skills (especially to new climbers)

- Teaching advanced climbing skills

- Supervising practice

- Disciplining students when needed

- Making arrangements for competitions (transportation, lodging, schedules, etc.)

- Belaying when necessary (avoid belaying if possible so that you can watch the student during practice and be available to help correct technique problems)

- Injury prevention/stretching

- Seeking out individual sponsorships (see Chapter 18)

- Keeping track of journal entries (making sure the student is doing it properly and often enough)

- Guest climbers—bringing in special instructors to help keep practice sessions exciting

- Volunteer coordination (lining up belayers when needed, getting extra help for mock competitions, etc.)

- Coordinating with gym route setters so that you can have specific climbs set up for practice

- Dealing with parents on discipline issues, getting parental support with unmotivated climbers, and other parental issues as they arise

- Chaperone (for climbers not accompanied by parents)

As you can see, there are many responsibilities involved in coaching. More questions will come up as you develop your program, so be prepared to work through those issues. As a coach, you need to have a plan and be flexible at the same time.

PARENT OR COACH?

Coaching your own child can create a difficult situation. You need to determine whether this is a workable arrangement. If you decide to coach your own child, she needs to understand that when you are at practice, she is a student and you are the coach. There should be no special considerations and no special treatment—especially if you are coaching more than one student at a time and your child happens to be one of them. It would be unfair to the other climber if your daughter constantly receives additional attention while the other student is being ignored. A parent is always a parent, but your priorities must change focus while at practice.

YOU ARE A TEACHER

Your student will be looking to you for guidance. Make sure you are organized enough to give it to him. If you do not have an answer, make a note to yourself and be sure to get back to your student with the proper response. First and foremost you are there to develop your student's climbing skills. Some exercises will not be well received, but it is still your responsibility to make sure the activities are being carried out correctly. You are not there to be a best friend, although you can be. Respect will be earned through an organized program that enables the student to acquire better climbing skills. If you allow a student to run all over you, you might be better off spending your time elsewhere.

HOW DO YOU WANT TO BE REMEMBERED?

Chances are you will be working with your student on a regular basis for a long period of time. Make sure you start off by earning his respect. You don't have to run your program like a military operation, but organization is key. Be punctual. Have a focus during each practice. Have a backup plan if something has changed in the gym that you didn't expect. Be consistent with your practices and training techniques. Change is good—but only if it is going in a positive direction.

LISTEN BEFORE YOU SPEAK

Sometimes your student's focus can change, even midseason. Make sure you are paying attention to the needs of each individual climber. If you are there for your student, she will be willing to work for you. Pay special attention to the dynamics between your climbers, especially if you have more than one climber during a session. Climbers consist of best friends, rivals, and acquaintances. If two best friends are having a problem, you will be the one to deal with it so that they can have a successful training session. Problems should be left at the door, but you may have to be the mediator if those problems enter the gym. Listen to both verbal and nonverbal clues. Don't let tensions build; solve issues as they come up.

SEPARATE THE PARENTS—YOU ARE THE COACH; YOU ARE IN CHARGE

One of the biggest issues that can come up with junior climbers is the parents. Keep the lines of communication open, but also be conscience of difficult parents. One example might be a parent putting unnecessary pressure on his child to be the best. You should not have to put up with unnecessary distractions during practice. If it is necessary to ask a parent to leave, then do it. Talk to your student first to make sure that it is an acceptable solution, but take action as soon as possible. Some parents try to make their children's accomplishments their own, and you may have to turn the focus away from the parent and back toward the child.

CONFIDENCE

It can also fall on your shoulders to help with the climbers self-esteem. If a climber always feels like the worst climber in the gym, you will need to find a way to encourage that student to continue despite their insecurities. If need be, private meetings with parents and students can be essential to everyone's mental health.

ISOLATE THE GYM

When your climbers come into the gym, they should leave everything but climbing outside the door, including any problems with school or relationships. The gym should be a place where your students can go to get away from everything else in their life. In order to concentrate completely on the workout at hand, climbing should be the only focus. Your student is at practice to climb, not to gossip or worry. Remind a troubled student that nothing in the outside world can be changed in the two to five hours of your session.

COACHING STYLES

Every coach has a different style of teaching, and every kid has a different style of learning that must be addressed for improvement to take place. Some students need visual stimulation; others need verbal prompting, so try to include both in your coaching.

As long as the sessions are under control, coaching styles can be flexible. If you need to be strict, make sure that you recognize when too much restriction hampers learning.

I once had a wonderful student that I pushed too far one day. Suddenly this bubbly student stopped talking. I realized I was pushing her too hard; she was actually close to tears. I laid off, and she finished the session. We talked about it during the next session, and I learned her limits as well as mine.

INTRODUCTION OF NEW EXERCISES

One basic way to introduce new exercises that will reach your students is by incorporating the formula below in your coaching style.

1. **Introduce the exercise.** Explain what the activity is and what it will do for the climber. Make sure your student understands exactly what you want her to work on.

2. **Demonstrate.** Make sure your climber understands the dynamics of what she needs to be doing. Don't just give an example without showing the sequence of how to complete what you expect. Break the moves down to show how each body part needs to move—the hands, hips, shoulders, and feet. Show the proper technique for what you want your student to accomplish. Provide good and bad examples, and exaggerate the movement so that the student can visualize it. Break it down into smaller parts if necessary.

3. **Explain.** Describe the move as you, or your model, demonstrate it. Explain what each body part should be doing and the steps involved in the exercise. Ask specifically if there are any questions before your student begins the activity so that she is clear on what is expected of her.

4. **Practice/guide**. Again, make sure your student understands the concept before having her practice the exercise. Watch each student individually. Verify that the activity is being carried out perfectly. Don't let a student slide on even a tiny aspect of the exercise, or it will never be done correctly. Remember, once something is learned it is difficult to relearn, so it must be properly reinforced the first time.

5. **Don't move on** to the next activity until each exercise is mastered.

HOW TO SELECT YOUR STUDENTS

There are many ways to decide whom you will coach and whom you won't. Some of this depends primarily on personalities. Some personalities do not click, and you should not force a bad situation. Certain coaches work well with some students and not well with others. Enter into a trial agreement with the student and make sure you can stick with it before committing to an entire season.

Following are some sample criteria for determining compatibility:

- Climbing ability

- Meeting students' goals (competing, training, etc.)

- Attitude (willingness to work together)

- Personal strengths the climber will bring to practice

- Individual climbing goals

- Determination

If you have the capacity to coach more than one student at a time, you need to decide if the students are compatible and able to work together. If one student is high energy and the other is blasé, you don't want the less-active student to bring down the other. Students should help push each other if they are training together, no matter what their individual ability level. There doesn't need to be competition between the students; they should be able to work on similar projects together without too much personality conflict.

Coaching two students with opposite strengths in a single session can help both students improve. For example, if one climber is an endurance climber and the other is a power climber, the power climber will gain endurance skills by watching the endurance climber's techniques, even on powerful routes. An endurance climber will have the ability to rest, whereas the power climber will be able to push through hard moves easier. Each climber can gain insight from the other's strengths, which makes for a nice combination.

If you are working with two climbers with the same strengths, they may tend to work what they are good at. You will need to diversify the workouts so that the climbers work on their weaknesses as much as their strengths. Weaknesses can keep a climber from finishing first in a competition, so turn those weaknesses into strengths to benefit the climber.

The Schedule

SET A SCHEDULE

You will want to work with individual students to determine a schedule that works best for them. If you are meeting more than once a week, you need to determine what schedule the climber needs to maintain so that you can make the most out of your training sessions together.

Physically, the best training schedule for most climbers is to climb two consecutive days and then take one to two days off. Following this schedule, the first day will be the more strenuous, focusing on power, and the second day will focus more on endurance. Typical after-school sessions should be a minimum of two hours—three is even better. A weekend session should be a minimum of three hours; four to five is even better. Ideally, to really improve, students should be climbing four days per week, and the number of days you take part in the schedule is up to you. If you are not at every session, you need to make sure that your student has a plan in place and sticks with it. You should be confident that your student is working on her personal program even when you are not there.

Sometimes it is nice to include "play days" in your schedule—times when your student can climb whatever she wants without working on specific exercises or training techniques. This will give her a chance to climb routes that she may not be working on during practice. These sessions can be scheduled by your student, and you do not need to be present.

LENGTH OF PRACTICE

A minimum of two hours is imperative for practice during the week. You can fig-ure the first fifteen minutes will be spent settling down, stretching, and explaining the objective for the training session. The next thirty minutes will be spent warm-ing up on the climbing wall. Thirty minutes is needed to get muscles warmed up and ready for "work." This leaves only an hour and fifteen minutes if you have a two-hour practice, which is not very much time for a training session. The average climber can get in about four hard routes during an hour—more if he is training for endurance or doing laps. When I am training kids, I like them to get a minimum of twelve routes in during a power/power-endurance session: three warm-ups, two medium to hard climbs, five or more climbs at the upper end of their ability level, and then the remainder of climbs to cool down. An endurance session should include a minimum of twenty routes, which will take more than two hours. You can arrange time for your training sessions according to the type of workout you have planned.

If you are coaching a student new to climbing, remember that she will need time for her body and skin to adjust to the strenuous activity of climbing. Start beginning students off with a *maximum* of two hours until they are physically pre-pared for more time on the wall.

TIME OFF

Some climbers choose to train just during the school year; others will train all year. Climbing can become an addiction, so make sure your students understand the need for breaks throughout the year to let their bodies recover. A few scheduled breaks are needed, regardless of how long your student practices during the year. For every six months of climbing, a climber should take between two and three consecutive weeks off from climbing but continue stretching and cross training.

As a training coach, you do not necessarily have to coach year around. Taking a few months off to climb with friends for recreation instead of training in the gym is great for the mental spirit.

Setting Goals You Can Live With

Young climbers will sometimes see "stars" and want to be the best climber in the gym in a short amount of time. As the coach, one goal is to make sure you can keep students motivated, even if their personal goal is not reached. In order to do this, you will need to set attainable goals—for you as well as your students.

To begin with, you should establish goals that you as a coach are able to achieve through a training schedule. If your goal is to have your student climbing 5.13 by the end of six months, and she is currently struggling on 5.11's, your goal will take a significant amount of time and effort to achieve. Are you willing to put in that amount of time?

Your students also will need to have achievable goals. Work with each individual climber that you are coaching and set short- and long-term goals. If necessary, dangle a carrot in front of students to encourage them to achieve what they are setting out to do. For example, if a student really wants to climb in the advanced category and is currently competing in the intermediate category, set a goal of onsighting a 5.12a. Once that goal is reached, she can compete in the advanced category. Try not to let your students get in over their heads and compete in an upper level category before they are ready. By earning it they will be more confident and perform better.

There will be more on goal-setting later in Chapter 14.

The Kids

AS INDIVIDUALS

The most impressive thing about working with young climbers is the kids themselves. Climbing can give kids a sport of their own—one in which they don't have to be compared with others and that they can excel in rather quickly based on their own abilities. Kids who climb have a strong sense of pride in their climbing because they are judged individually on their own merits. Climbers tend to be extremely dedicated to their sport and typically want to excel.

One of the most wonderful aspects of the sport is the relationships that develop among climbers. It is a small, tight-knit community across the United States and even the world. Because they share an interest in climbing, some kids will gravitate toward other kids they normally would never have associated with. An advanced climber can climb with a beginner and not be held back. You can pair up students of all abilities (as long as they have the proper belay skills), and give the kids the opportunity to climb with others in the gym. It is important for climbers to support and encourage one another—in practice and in competitions.

DEDICATION

The dedication these kids bring to the gym can be extreme. Make sure your students are not pushing so hard that they develop overuse injuries in the tendons or muscles. You can use their dedication by allowing the kids to push themselves to their maximum climbing ability, while at the same time staying healthy.

DISCIPLINE

As a coach, you will be responsible for discipline during practice, and that may include setting rules for performance outside training sessions. Some coaches prefer to draw up a set of rules for their students to follow; others are more lenient and make up the rules as they go along.

Following are some basic issues to consider when determining your rules:

- Missing practice—you are dedicating your time, and if you have a student who doesn't show up to practice, what are the results of that action? Do you charge for the session anyway? Give a warning?

- Outside issues such as schoolwork and parental control

- Tardiness

- Not following directions

- Acting up

Once you have determined the rules, you need to decide what the punishment will be for any infraction. Problems with students must be addressed as soon as possible. If a rule is broken and becomes an ongoing issue, you may decide to discontinue coaching that climber. This will be up to you, but you will need to stand your ground once a decision has been made.

Remember that you are in control. Make sure your students understand that they cannot take advantage of you. If you are having problems with a student, have him sign a contract with rules and disciplinary actions written out in detail.

Activities and Sample Schedules

PRACTICE PLAN

1. **Warm-up: 10 minutes.** This is done on the ground to warm up the muscles: jumping jacks, running, games, etc.—any activity that will get the body moving and the muscles warmed up.

2. **Stretch: 10–15 minutes.** Remember not to stretch until the muscles are warm. Make sure the hands, fingers, and upper and lower body all get stretched. Vary stretching exercises from practice to practice so that your student doesn't get bored. Stretching is the best way to prevent injury.

3. **Warm up on the wall/bouldering: 20–30 minutes.** Have your student warm up on routes that have been designated especially for her based on her climbing ability. During this warm-up time, the student should try to complete at least three warm-up routes, developing a slight "pump" with the muscles in the now warmed up upper body. Students should not fall on any move during their warm-up; falling indicates that the routes are too difficult. Kids tend to warm up too quickly, which creates an increased risk of injury. The goal of warm-up climbs is to move the body and to get the muscles warmed up, not to bag onsights! See the chart below for reasonable warm-ups based on onsight and redpoint abilities.

ONSIGHT LEVEL	WARM-UP (2–3 climbs)	POST WARM-UP (2–3 climbs)	REDPOINT LEVEL
5.8 to 5.9	5.6 to 5.7	5.8	5.10-
5.10- to 5.10	5.8	5.9	5.10+
5.11+ to 5.12a	5.10 to 5.10+	5.11- to 5.11	5.12b/c
5.12b/c	5.10+ to 5.11-	5.11 to 5.12a	5.13-

4. **Practice.** Plan sessions ahead of time—concentrate on only one or two aspects of technique per practice. Resist the urge to introduce too many exercises in one session, because introducing too many techniques or exercises will

promote mediocre climbing. Explain and demonstrate the exercises. I will usually have a maximum of two exercises planned for any given practice; if we
only get to one, that's okay as long as it is done to perfection.

5. **Recap/Journal: final 5–10 minutes of practice.** Make sure your student
keeps an individual journal, which is written in after each training session. Sit
down with your student and talk about what worked and what didn't. Give
assignments for climbing sessions outside of practice. Have the climber write
down thoughts during those sessions when you are not there so that you can
refer back to the journal to see what he accomplished.

Journaling after a long training session. Photo: Rod Willard

Use the following chart to plan out a week's practice session or modify it to
plan a month of sessions.

Practice Planning Chart

Student Name				
Day and Date				
Training Day	1st	2nd	3rd	4th
Focus Activity (power, power-endurance, endurance, or bouldering)				
Exercises:				
Number of Climbs:				
Problems/Techniques to Work On:				
Homework for Student:				

Chapter 4:
Identifying Weaknesses Through Evaluation

One of the easiest ways to determine where to start coaching any new student is to watch her climb. I will typically watch a student on a few climbs while filling out an evaluation form so that I can get a good feel for her ability and determine what she should be working on.

Using the evaluation form in this chapter is a good starting point to begin determining the areas your student needs to work on. You need to be extremely picky in this evaluation—mark down each imperfection that you see. Watch every move closely and evaluate several different types of climbs. Make sure you mark on the evaluation which climbs suit the student and which ones he struggles on. This is important for figuring out what the climber's strengths and weaknesses are.

Once the evaluation is done, chose one or two major weaknesses and have the student concentrate only on those. Don't give the student too many areas to work on, or nothing will improve significantly. Give him two objectives to work on until they are perfected (usually a minimum of a couple of weeks), and then pick a couple more objectives/weaknesses. After all the techniques have improved, then you can perform another evaluation to determine more weaknesses.

The evaluation itself needs to be done without distractions. You should only concentrate on the climber you are evaluating; someone else should belay. Walk around the base of the climb so that you can see the climber from all angles. Look at the evaluation form ahead of time so that you know what to look for. This way you can complete an evaluation in only a few climbs. Is the climber always "pulling" through moves? Perhaps her arms are bent too much, and she isn't pushing with her legs. If on lead, is the climber fumbling clips, but only with the left hand? Is the climber backstepping, yet her hips are facing the wall? Maybe she needs to have a refresher course on backstepping and the perfect position for maximum leg power. Make sure to designate these types of observations on the evaluation form.

Evaluations can also be videotaped. When using this method, it is best to evaluate the student during the climb while someone else is videotaping. This allows you to make notes during the climb. When viewing the tape with the climber, you can actually point out the weaknesses so that the student can see what she is doing wrong. Video is a good reinforcer of your evaluation. During some evaluations the climber will not believe that she had fumbled clips for example, but when she sees on video that she dropped the rope twice on one clip, she will understand what you are talking about. Video can also be used to figure out why a climber is falling during a redpoint or onsight climb. He will be able to see for himself what is going wrong and sometimes be able to pinpoint what needs to change. If possible, videotape during one of the first practices and then about once a month. Video recordings can be used to show improvement of technique over a period of time.

The Evaluation Explained

Pushing with legs. This will be obvious from the motion of the body. If the body shoots upward, the leg muscles are probably being utilized. Most beginning climbers pull with their arms and let the legs follow without really initiating the leg muscles for upward motion. *The legs should initiate all movements.*

Quiet feet. There should be no sound at all from the feet/shoes. If the climber is not watching his feet, there will be an obvious sound because he doesn't know where his feet are landing and is not placing them carefully. Chances are the feet are landing randomly on holds. When a climber is *not* watching his feet, he will have to go by "feel" or "sound" to know if they are actually landing on a foothold. By having quiet feet, he will be more aware of his foot movements. He will have to watch his foot from the time it leaves one hold to the time it is set (carefully) on the next foothold. Noisy footwork indicates that the climber is not confident enough to put full pressure on his shoe.

Small steps. Two small steps are always better than one big one. If a climber is stepping too high, the arm muscles will have to be activated to pull the body

THE EVALUATION

	GOOD	NEEDS WORK	
LEGS/LOWER BODY	☐	☐	Pushing with legs
	☐	☐	Quiet feet
	☐	☐	Small steps
	☐	☐	Moving feet on wall (tapping, etc.)
	☐	☐	Soft foot placement
	☐	☐	Foot stable on hold
	☐	☐	Looking at feet
	☐	☐	Confidence in feet
BODY POSITION	☐	☐	Pulling with arms (too much)
	☐	☐	Straight arms
	☐	☐	Too stretched out for holds
	☐	☐	Gripping holds lightly
	☐	☐	Three points of contact
	☐	☐	"Set" position before movement
	☐	☐	Balance/shifting weight
	☐	☐	Backstep
	☐	☐	Hips (backstep position)
	☐	☐	Body position (hips in/shoulders out)
ADVANCED MOVEMENT	☐	☐	Static movement
	☐	☐	Dynamic movement
	☐	☐	Confidence in holds
	☐	☐	Breathing
	☐	☐	Relaxed climbing
	☐	☐	Relaxed resting
	☐	☐	Accuracy
	☐	☐	Timing
	☐	☐	Power
	☐	☐	Endurance
	☐	☐	Recovery
	☐	☐	Body tension
	☐	☐	Memorization

The climber should concentrate on the following weaknesses first:

1)

2)

The climber exhibits the following strengths:

Additional comments:

higher than the foot. If a climber is flexible through the hips, high steps will not be a problem. For 90 percent of the climbers out there, however, big steps cause more effort to be exerted on the upper body to gain upward movement. Encourage your student to smear a foot on the wall or take two small steps rather than high stepping.

Moving feet on wall (tapping, etc.) This can be obvious just by looking at the climber's shoes. If the sole is worn down on the upper part of the shoe near the toe area, the climber is probably dragging his foot. The other obvious indicator is the actual sound of the foot tapping up the wall for balance. If the climber is "tapping" or "dragging" his foot on the wall, chances are he needs to work on balance—shifting the weight completely over one foot while moving the other.

Soft foot placement. Foot movements should be very careful and delicate. The foot should not be slammed down onto footholds but rather carefully placed, and then the weight should shift over onto the foothold.

Foot stable on hold. The foot should be balanced on the hold, typically with the front end of the shoe. The foot should not move once there is weight on the foothold—no bouncing, shifting, or readjusting.

Looking at feet. Anytime the foot is being moved on the wall, the climber should have her eyes on that foot. The eyes do not leave the foot until it is stable on the next foothold and there is weight on it. If the climber is not looking at her foot, she will not have the confidence to use her feet as efficiently as possible. If a climber is watching her feet, there will not be any sound as the shoe is set on the foothold. If you hear a sound, she is not watching her feet!

Confidence in feet. If the climber is using his legs efficiently and really pushing with his toes, he is probably confident in his footwork. If he is not pushing with his toes and seems to hesitate using his legs/feet, he is probably not trusting them and should work on watching his feet.

Pulling with arms (too much). If the climber's arms are always bent during upward motion, he is probably pulling too much with the upper body. Climbing movement should incorporate the lower body initiating the movement, with the upper body for balance. Many climbers forget about the lower body and don't use it to help with upward motion. You can tell when someone is pulling too much with the upper body if she is close to the wall, feet skating out from under the body, and muscles in the back/shoulders/neck engaged. The elbows will begin to raise upward as the climber gets pumped.

Pulling too much with the arms wastes energy! Keep the arms straight when moving the feet up. Photo: Stewart Green

Straight arms. The arms should be straight whenever the climber is resting, clipping, or making movements that incorporate the lower body, especially when backstepping. The goal is to not always have straight arms but to use them as efficiently as possible. When climbing regular routes, the elbows will have to bend during certain moves, such as lock offs. However, the shoulders and hips should be used

The proper rest position—left arm is straight, right arm is dangling. The climber is not looking at the rest of the route. Shoulders are relaxed and away from the wall, putting the weight on the feet. Photo: Rod Willard

whenever possible to gain height on the wall without bending the elbows. When the shoulders and hips are used to move the body, the movement becomes more efficient and the muscles in the arms/shoulders don't have to do all of the work.

Too stretched out for holds. If the climber is constantly looking up for handholds, reaching, pulling, and then moving up the legs, she is probably getting too stretched out or extended. The problem with this is that in order to get out of a stretched-out position, the climber must pull with the upper body to bring up the feet. It is better technique to move up the legs first and then reach for the next handhold.

Reaching high for the next hold, Brett Spencer-Green is rather extended for his next move. Photo: Stewart Green

Gripping holds lightly. Holds should be held with the least amount of pressure possible. If you can see white around the climber's knuckles, he is probably holding on too tight and should try to relax his grip. Holding onto holds too tight also makes the elbows bend, and brings the biceps unintentionally into play. The tighter the grip on a hold, the more muscle is being used. On a steep wall you can have the climber hang—straight arms, no feet on the wall—and try to hold on as loosely as possible. This should help your student understand that friction will hold him on and that he doesn't need a death grip.

Light grip explained: Hold your hand out loosely in front of you, and then clench your fist tightly. You should see your elbow bend, which is an indication that the biceps are being activated. When climbing, those muscles should be used as little as possible.

Three points of contact. In order for a climber to be balanced, she should always have three points of contact with the wall. Those three points should be a combination of hands and feet—not knees, head, hip, or any other body part. Any time one point of contact is being moved, the other three points should remain stable with equal pressure. In other words, if the climber is moving a hand, both feet and the other hand should not move. If a climber has only two points of contact (moving a hand and a foot at the same time), balance will be compromised, forcing the climber to hold on tighter or make unnecessary adjustments to get back into balance. If a foot comes off as the climber reaches for a hold with a hand, the feet probably need to be higher on the wall.

Balanced with three points of contact, and chalking up, Erin Axtell has her eyes on the next move as she onsights a route in Imst, Austria. Photo: Craig Axtell

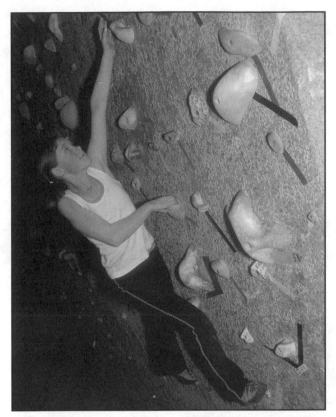

Catherine Oja sets her position completely before touching the next hold—this assures that she will be able to reach it without jumping or adjusting her body. Photo: Stewart Green

"Set" position before movement. The climber should always be balanced before making a move. If the climber "sways" or "pops up" to reach for a hold, he is probably out of balance before making the move. The position should be set prior to making the move so that he "sticks" the next hold without having to adjust the body. One way to envision this is to have the climber imagine holding the next hold. What position would his body be in at that point? Now have the climber get into that position *before* reaching for the next hold so that no additional movement needs to be made after he has made the move.

Balance/shifting weight. As a climber advances up the wall, she should be balanced at all times, anticipating where her body needs to be and shifting her weight before making a move. Weight shifts should be initiated from the lower body, with the toes—not the arms—pulling the body into position when a shift needs to be made. The arms should be used to keep the body balanced but not to shift the body's weight.

Under the tutelage of a coach, Katie Brown does a backstep during a U.S. Climbing Team training camp. Photo: Stewart Green

As Hunter reaches up with her left hand, the coach turns her hips so that she is in the ideal backstep position.
Photo: Stewart Green

Backstep. This move is made by putting one hip against the wall and reaching up with the inside hand. The climber is actually facing perpendicular to the wall, with the side of the body against the wall.

Hips (backstep position). You will need to be looking at the direction of the climber's hips in the backstep position. If both hip bones are facing the wall during a backstep, the climber will need to turn so that one hip is flush with the wall and the other is straight out. When backstepping, the climber's hips should be facing away from the wall to form a T position. The wall forms the top of the T, and the hips/body form the base of the T coming straight out from the wall. If the hips are facing the wall, the climber needs to push on the back leg to turn his hips away from the wall. In a partial backstep position (with the hips facing the wall), the legs are not being used as efficiently as possible. The hips must be turned for the lower body to be able to initiate the upward movement. Arching the back can help keep body tension on the lower part of the body, keeping weight on the feet.

Body position (hips in/shoulders out). Any time the climber is facing the wall while contemplating a move, the arms should be straight, shoulders away

On an overhanging wall, it is especially important for the climber to lean away from the wall with her shoulders and push into the wall with her hips, forcing the weight over her feet. Photo: Stewart Green

from the wall, and hips arched into the wall. With the hips into the wall, there will be pressure on the legs—taking the weight off of the upper body. Extra pressure on the feet will keep the shoes from sliding off footholds. With the shoulders away from the wall and the back arched, the climber will be in a bit of a rest position. With the arms straight in a resting position, the climber has a vantage point from which to look around for handholds. When looking for footholds, the arms can remain straight and the hips can be pulled out away from the wall. As soon as the new footholds are located, the feet can come up and the hips return close to the wall.

Have you heard or used the term *"get close to the wall"*? Most people use this term incorrectly, and it is usually interpreted as getting the entire body as close to the wall as possible. In actuality, if the *entire* body is close to the wall, it is impossible to see where to go, and the arms will have to be bent to keep the body close. This position expends unnecessary energy in the biceps/upper body. Only the hips should be close to the wall.

Static movement. Static climbing means the climber is not using momentum to get to the next hold. Climbers who are always in balance are probably climbing statically and are not using dynamic movement to get to the next hold. Static climbing is important because the climber is in balance. Nearly every move can be done statically by the climber with three points of contact. However, some climbers tend to climb too statically and waste energy by not using momentum to get to the next hold. If a climber tends to lock off every single move, or pull very slowly between moves, he may want to become a more dynamic climber. If a climber is too dynamic—always jumping for holds—and tends to lose her balance a lot, she should work to become more static. Some moves are better performed dynamically to save energy; some moves are delicate and should be carried out statically so that balance is not sacrificed.

Dynamic movement. The opposite of static movement, dynamic movement is using momentum to make a move by initiating a movement from the lower body. Dynamic movement saves energy in the upper body if it is carried out in a controlled fashion. Watch for accuracy when a climber is using dynamic movement. He should be fully aware of body position during the entire movement, not over- or undershooting for a hold. If the movement is not controlled, it is possible to miss the hold and be unable to control the fall. In a true "dyno," the entire body is out of contact of the wall—zero points of contact. Dynos can be taught, but for most climbers learning how to move the body in a dynamic movement is more important than being able to throw the entire body up the wall with no points of contact.

Confidence in holds. Most climbers will grab a hold and use it, but some climbers tend to feel around, looking for the most secure place to hold. If a climber tends to "pump" holds and feel around, she is flexing the muscles with each "pump" and wasting energy. Have her perform the simple exercise of placing the hand on a hold and using it in whatever way the hold is grabbed. This should help the climber become more confident on the hold if she is unable to shift her hand. Often a new hold can throw off a climber, but she must learn to have confidence in every hold she grabs. When climbing outside, nearly every hold is unfamiliar; that is something climbers must adjust to. When a climber is onsighting a route, holds will be unfamiliar, and the climber needs to have confidence to reach out and grab a hold without having to feel around for the most secure part. A climber should feel comfortable with any hold she has in her hand, but some climbers will not feel secure on certain types of holds. The important thing is to work the climber's weaknesses and make every hold comfortable.

Breathing. While breathing is not always easy to determine from the ground, if a climber becomes tight as he moves up the wall, chances are you can tell he is not breathing properly. It is important for the climber to continue breathing in nice steady, deep breaths so that the muscles receive enough oxygen to recover. As the climber moves up the wall, he should be visibly breathing, and you should be able see the shoulders rise and fall during rest stances. If the climber gets to the top of the wall and you see him taking deep breaths as he is being lowered, you may want to work with him on breathing techniques while moving up the wall.

Relaxed climbing. As the climber moves up the wall, the body should "flow," and any jerking motions are an indication that the climber is holding tension in her body. The climber should move smoothly through the motions of each position. A major indication of relaxed climbing is the shoulders; they should be relaxed at all times, never tight or held rigid. If you see the elbows raising up behind or the shoulders joining the ears, the climber needs to learn relaxation techniques.

Relaxed resting. Again, a major indication of relaxation is no tension in the shoulders. When a climber is resting on the wall, the upper body and shoulder muscles should be relaxed. The body should be relaxed over the legs—knees bent

While reading the route, Ian Spencer-Green is in the perfect rest position—his weight is low, his shoulders are back and relaxed, and his resting hand is aimed at the floor.
Photo: Stewart Green

so that the weight of the body can rest on the feet—arms should be straight and shoulders relaxed. Resting should also incorporate breathing, usually at least three deep breaths during each rest stance is sufficient, but sometimes time allows only one. If the climber does not look comfortable while resting, she may need to work on finding better rest positions. Resting is a chance to recover and relax the muscles so that they will be refreshed for the remainder of the climb. Try to get the climber to look down at the ground and open up the shoulders, which accomplishes two things: It relaxes the neck, and it keeps the climber from looking at the rest of the route and tensing up in anticipation of upcoming moves.

Accuracy. When reaching for a handhold, the climber should be able to determine exactly where to grab it. If he is overshooting the hold (reaching too high) or undershooting (missing the hold completely), then he needs to keep focus on the hold longer so that the hand lands precisely on the correct place on the hold.

It is always better, however, to overshoot a hold than to undershoot and miss completely.

Timing. During a climb there will be sections that are more difficult and sections that are less difficult. As the climber moves through a climb, she needs to determine which sections require more accuracy and perhaps slower movement and which sections she can move through quickly so that less energy is expended. The climber needs to determine what pace is necessary for each section of the climb.

Typically an easier section of a climb is climbed slowly so that each move becomes a rest and is used to the ultimate advantage. The climber will probably have to "push it" through the crux so that the smaller holds can be used quickly, then released.

Power. Somewhat difficult to determine during a quick evaluation, power should be evaluated separately by using short boulder problems. You can see if a climber has power if he is able to really push through a couple of moves that are at or over his maximum climbing ability. Some climbers are unable to just push through moves, trying instead to make moves slowly and with too much static movement. Powerful moves will need to take all the climber's determination to get through. If the climber doesn't grunt or look like he is working hard, then the move is probably not difficult enough. If a climber is unable to do big or powerful moves, he should probably work on a system or campus board to develop power.

Endurance. One of the key elements of climbing fitness is having the endurance to complete a climb. If a climber gets within a few holds of the top of a climb and cannot complete the last few moves, she needs to work on endurance. Another alternative to building up endurance is learning how to rest properly. Sometimes the difference between winning and losing a competition is one hold— endurance can make or break that one more move.

Recovery. This is the basic muscle recovery during a rest. Some climbers will be able to shake their hand one time and regain their muscular power; other climbers will need a ten-second rest on the wall. Each climber needs to know how long his recovery period is so that he can recover to his optimum power before continuing on a route. Recovery also includes the time it takes to recover after climbing a difficult problem and before the climber takes another lap or attempts a redpoint. This recovery time can range anywhere between five and twenty minutes. Some ways to help recovery are drinking water, stretching out the muscles, building up the muscles, and working on endurance.

Body tension. Using three points of contact, proper body tension means keeping equal amounts of pressure on all three points of contact at all times. The most important aspect of body tension is the core of the body (abs). If the climber is on a steep wall and her abs are not strong enough, she will struggle to hold her legs/feet on the wall. With good body tension, the climber's feet never lose contact with the wall. When body tension is released and the feet come off, the climber should not fight the swing/momentum to bring her feet back onto the wall. Instead the feet should swing away and then back onto the wall without fighting it. Body tension is especially important during the backstep position. If there is no body tension on the lower body (no pressure on the legs/feet), the climber will be unable to use her body to its ultimate ability.

Memorization. When redpointing or onsighting routes, knowing where to go

Katie Brown demonstrates excellent body tension with her hips up and keeping three points of contact on a steep wall—all while watching the draw she is clipping.
Photo: Stewart Green

With his lack of body tension, Chris Sharma looks like he's going to come off when his leg cuts away from the wall.
Photo: Stewart Green

is almost as important as being able to do the moves, especially on difficult routes. If a climber gets confused or goes the wrong direction, it is possible to get off route. Reading a route ahead of time—with the entire body—is almost like climbing the route. Once a climber has climbed a route once, the muscles should know the moves, making the move easier to perform the next time. Memorizing routes can come in handy outside as well as inside. If a climber has good memorization skills and knows exactly where to go before he leaves the ground, he will not waste valuable energy stopping on the route and trying to figure out where he needs to go.

Self-evaluation

After each climb, have the climber evaluate where he had trouble, why he was unable to complete a move, or why he fell. Take the time to identify the problem. Have the climber answer the following questions so that he can pinpoint the point of failure.

- Did you lose mental concentration?

- Were your feet where they needed to be?

- Were you pumped?

- Could you see what needed to be done and just couldn't do it?

Taking the time to have the climber evaluate his own performance will be the biggest factor in improvement. Barriers cannot be broken down until they are identified. Make sure your students are keeping a journal of each climb so that they can pinpoint what areas need improvement. Typically, with the help of a journal, your students will find one or two main reasons for repeatedly failing on any given climb. Once they have those areas pinpointed, it will be easy to find solutions and work on the problems.

Once you have determined what the problem is—you will usually see a pattern develop during the self-evaluation—you can now decide what the climber needs to work on to improve. If the reason the climber fell was because she was "pumped," she needs to work on endurance. If the climber fell because she couldn't reach a hold, "the climb was too reachy," she needs to move her feet up higher and work on footwork (see Chapter 5). If the climber fell because she lost mental concentration—saw the move and just couldn't pull it off—she needs to do the "holding exercise" (see Chapter 5) and work on visualization. With each problem that is identified, determine what needs to be done for the climber. The self-evaluation forms on the following pages will help in this task.

Note: If the climber did not fall during the self-evaluation climbs, she is not pushing herself hard enough for a proper evaluation.

Student Self-evaluation Log   Date:

Climb #	Rating of Climb/location/ description/type of climb (sloppy/steep/slabby, etc.)	Why did you fall or have trouble? Be descriptive (too tired, hard move, couldn't commit to the move, reachy, feet too high/low, made the move the second try, pumped, lost mental concentration, etc.)	How difficult was the climb for you? (easy, moderate, hard)
1			
2			
3			
4			
5			
6			
7			
8			
9			
10			

After you have completed your climbs, go back and evaluate the number of times you fell for the same reason. There will probably be a pattern (always pumped, too reachy, etc.). Then work with your coach for ways to correct the problem.

Self-evaluation Questions

1) If you fell, or had trouble on a particular move, explain why. Examples: Pumped, not pushing yourself, foot slipped, type of hold (pinch, crimper, sloper, etc.), confidence, don't know the move, reachy, incorrect reading, scared to move, fall, clip, etc.

_____
_____
_____
_____
_____
_____

2) Explain how you felt at the completion of the climb. Examples: Pumped, good, confident, weak, powerful, tired, fluid, etc. *(All emotions are valid for a proper evaluation.)*

_____
_____
_____
_____
_____
_____

3) Based on this climb, what is the most important thing you feel you should work on? Examples: Endurance, technique, clipping, footwork, breathing, relaxing, resting, etc.

_____
_____
_____
_____
_____

4) What type of climb/problem was this? Was this type of climb easy or difficult for you?

_____
_____
_____
_____
_____
_____

Chapter 5:
Exercises to Work on Technique

Any time a climber is not climbing smoothly, technique should be the first area to work on to help that climber become more fluid. The following exercises may become monotonous, but if your student is able to achieve perfection, her climbing ability will improve without even working on other aspects, such as power and endurance. If nothing else, she will *look* better when she climbs!

I recommend doing each exercise for at least thirty minutes continuously per session, for a duration of three to five weeks. Pick one to two exercises and work on them exclusively until perfect, and then move on to another couple of exercises for the next month. A climber can still do routes, but he should be concentrating on the given exercise at all times. Paying dues upfront will make your student a better climber, without having to relearn techniques later.

Footwork Exercises

QUIET CLIMBING
Technique: footwork
Concept: Climbing without any noise from the feet. To do this, the climber needs to watch his feet until they are firmly set on the hold. This will help him to put his feet exactly where he wants them, instead of "skating" off or "slamming" onto footholds. It will help him concentrate on his footwork so that he will place his feet deliberately. Be sure he sets his feet firmly—shifting his weight over the foot—before moving to his next point of contact. Do not let him take his eyes off of his feet until they are weighted.

Activity: Have the student climb on easy routes, preferably during the warm-up. He should climb the routes (or boulder) concentrating only on silent climbing. In the beginning, it helps to walk behind the climber and tell him when you hear his feet. *Any* sound is too much. After awhile the climber will become tuned in to any sound from his feet and know when he is not watching them. This exercise should be used at the beginning of *every* training session, as good habits will follow the climber throughout the remainder of the workout until quiet feet become ingrained.

SMEARING AND FLAGGING

Technique: footwork

Concept: Sometimes there are no footholds available in the exact place needed to make a move. Smearing makes use of the wall texture in the absence of a foothold and can actually be considered a "foothold" if done correctly.

Putting pressure on the sole of the shoe, this climber smears against the wall. Photo: Stewart Green

The left foot is actually considered a point of contact—even though it is not touching a hold, it is keeping Hunter in balance as she flags with it. Photo: Stewart Green

Proper smearing position is to have the smearing foot directly in front of the body, as high as necessary to get as much rubber from the shoe on the wall as possible; around knee level is ideal. If a climber smears too low on the wall, there will not be enough friction/pressure to hold the foot on the wall, and it will skate out from under the body. The smearing foot must have weight on it to make it stick. If the foot is out to the side—instead of directly in front of the climber—it will also skate out and lose contact with the surface.

Flagging is the use of a foot, pointed out to the side, to keep the body from swinging, swaying, or being out of balance when there is not a foothold. No foothold is used, but the flagging foot is considered a "point of contact."

Activity: On toprope, choose one foot for the climber to use on footholds. Only smear (using the texture of the wall, no holds) and flag (point the toe out to the side for balance) with the other foot. This will teach her to use her body position to balance without always having both feet on a hold. Have your student practice this exercise with each foot. Have the climber go to the top of the wall smearing and flagging with the right foot, lower to the ground, and then smear and flag with the left foot.

Sometimes it is not necessary, and can be a hindrance, to have both feet on holds. On regular moves, check her body position to see if it could be in better balance by flagging or smearing instead of having both feet on a hold.

OUTSIDE EDGE

Technique: footwork

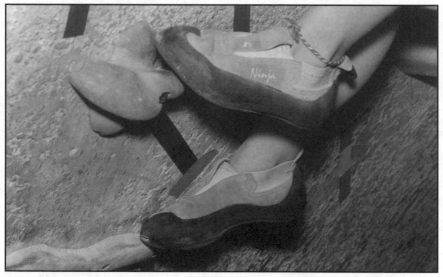

With both feet pointing in the same direction, this climber uses the outside edge of her right foot on a hold. Photo: Stewart Green

Concept: When traversing, have the climber point both feet in the same direction—outside edge of one foot, inside edge of the other. This position uses a very strong part of the foot and leg (the outer edge) and will help turn the body to a strong position (with one hipbone against the wall). Make sure the climber uses one foot (the back one) to "push" through a move and the other toe to "pull" onto the next hold. This is essentially using the "backstep" position.

Activity: On a bouldering wall, have the climber face to the right. He will put the left outside edge of his back foot and his right inside edge on the wall. Now have the climber maintain this position and move forward 20 feet and then backward. When done, have the climber face left and go frontward and backward again.

Activity 2: Pick five holds low on the wall, each on a different angle. The climber starts on one hold with the body low (knees bent, arms straight) and then, using the outside edge of one foot, pushes upward in the backstep position. Have your student practice on each leg five times—pushing upward with the back leg and arching the back before returning to the start position—so that the movement is felt through the hips and legs. The climber doesn't have to reach for an actual hold but can just stretch the arm straight up without grabbing any holds before returning to the start position. Once the climber is able to do each leg comfortably, have him switch from one side to the other (right backstep, return to the start with the arms straight, and then left backstep). This repetition will help you pinpoint the exact movement for your student. You may need to physically place his hips in the correct position for each move. Repeat on each of the holds you have picked throughout the gym.

FOOTWORK

Technique: footwork

Concept: When bouldering or climbing, set up moves so that the climber places his feet once and then makes a couple of moves with the upper body. This will help eliminate some of the questions as to where the feet need to be for a move. By placing the feet once, then making the next few hand or body shifting moves, the climber can build up his endurance by not making unnecessary moves. Climbers should plan their body position ahead for the next move so that they don't have to decide where to go in the middle of the move. They should be in position to complete a move before starting it.

Activity: Have a climber traverse a wall. Count the foot movements. Have her traverse the same wall using the same hands if possible, and eliminate half the foot movements. Often one foot can be used to pull onto a foothold and then push off, instead of relocating to another hold.

PUSH

Technique: legwork

Concept: The legs are much stronger than the arms, so using the legs to push up the wall will save upper body strength. On any steep or overhanging wall, the legs must be used to push the climber through the moves to save arm strength.

Activity: While having your student climb on an easy route, have him concentrate on using his feet/legs to push his body up the climb. Have him say "push" out loud whenever he engages his leg muscles. He will actually use more leg muscles—which are much stronger than the arms—when he is saying the word *push*. It is almost as if saying it out loud creates a direct connection to the leg muscles so that they respond by contracting and "pushing" upward. When the workout is over, the climber should feel as though his leg muscles have been used.

Activity 2: Pick five good holds on the wall close to the ground, but spread out and at different angles. Have your student use each hold to "push" (saying it out loud) with the legs five times in a row. After the student pushes upward with the legs, she should sink back down to a starting position of arms straight, legs bent. Repeat on each hold.

BAD FEET

Technique: footwork

Concept: Using bad footholds is a necessity, especially as climbs increase in difficulty. If a climber is unable to trust her feet, she will not put weight on a bad hold and will grip the handholds tighter.

Activity: When training to improve footwork, one surefire method to get your climber to use horrible feet and improve her body tension is to have her boulder on a minimally steep wall (10 to 25 degrees) using only bolt holes (the T-nut holes that are in the wall without any holds attached) for feet. She will probably have to use better handholds, as the feet will be very tenuous, but by using only the bolt holes for feet, she will have to learn to use her entire body to take advantage of the holes. One way to start this exercise is by using only bolt holes to start a boulder problem (the first two footholds are bolt holes). Once the climber has mastered getting off the ground and making the first move with bad feet, move on to designate bolt holes only for the right foot, regular footholds for the left. Once that is mastered, switch to the left. When both feet are mastered, make up easy boulder problems that incorporate only bolt holes for both feet. The climber will have to use the bolt holes carefully and fully weight them in order to complete the problems.

Body Work Exercises

STRAIGHT ARM CLIMBING

Technique: body movement

Concept: Keeping the arms straight during upward movement will prevent the climber from using power and muscle strength to make moves. It will also rest the arm muscles as the student is climbing and help her understand how to move her body without using muscles, thereby saving strength. Straight arms help with balance when shifting with the lower body and using the hands to push, instead of pull, up the wall. The goal is not always to have the arms straight while climbing, but rather to have the arms straight (relaxed) any time the climber is moving her feet.

Climbing with the arms straight takes concentration—make sure the arms don't bend at all, even during upward movement.
Photo: Stewart Green

Activity: Have the climber do easy routes without bending her elbows. If necessary, you can get large tubes and slide them over the climber's arms to prevent her elbows from bending. Sometimes climbers do not realize that they are bending their elbows, so let them know each time they bend them for this exercise.

BODY TENSION

Technique: body movement

Concept: The climber should know at all times where his body is and where it needs to be to complete a move. If he releases his body tension, what happens to his feet? Do they come off the wall? If his body is not held into the wall with his core body strength (abs), he might not have the extension or body tension to reach the next hold. If his feet come off the wall, causing his body to swing, he may lose his balance. Be aware of "overgripping." When the feet come off the wall, have him incorporate body tension instead, especially in overhanging areas. Have the climber be as efficient as possible with his footwork and movement—extra moves expend more energy.

Working body tension, Stefan Hibl pulls with his toe onto the hold the coach points out.
Photo: Stewart Green

Activity: Pick a large handhold that both hands will fit on (preferably on an overhanging wall). Have the climber hold on, with his legs dangling. With a stick, point out a foothold for the right foot. The climber needs to place his foot on that hold without swinging away. To stick the move, he must pull into the wall with his hip and place the foot on the hold. Let the climber come back to neutral (feet dangling), and then point out a left foothold. Continue to point holds in different positions on the wall, about five to ten movements per side. The footholds should be high, low, wide, and narrow for variety. Each foot placement should be done with quiet feet. (See "One Foot Climbing" later in this chapter for another excellent body tension exercise.)

STEP/STEP/REACH/REACH

Technique: legwork

Concept: A fundamental mistake that most climbers make is always to look up for handholds, move their hands, and then worry about their feet as an afterthought. Proper technique is to locate the next handhold, move the feet up, push with the legs, and then reach for that handhold.

Activity: The climber needs to pick a handhold first—but not reach for it. The climber then steps up with his feet so that he can reach the hold without "pulling" with his arms. Both feet must come up before the climber is allowed to reach for the next hold. "Step, step, reach, reach" is a habit that must be developed. Do not let the climber move his hands until his feet have advanced on the wall. Have the climber do this exercise during one entire training session. If the climber is having trouble with the basic theory, have him verbally say *"step, step"* with each foot movement, and then *"reach, reach"* as he moves his hands.

HOLDING/LOCKING OFF

Technique: body position

Concept: Some climbers tend to rush through moves and do not commit to a move, even though they can see what needs to be done. To improve technique, the climber needs to completely establish her position on the wall before committing to a move.

Activity: Have the climber pick a route that is an easy climb for her. (She shouldn't have to struggle on any of the moves.) She must climb the route with a three- to five-second pause before each handhold is grasped. The goal is to do this without struggling, getting out of balance, or having to pull too much with her hands.

Lock off and reach—Ian Spencer-Green focuses on the next hold. Photo: Stewart Green

The climber should read the route from the ground before tying in. Once the climber has the first handhold and both feet off the ground, she must establish herself—move up the feet, get into the proper position—and pause before grabbing the next hold. During the pause, the hand should be at the hold, the body perfectly still. She should count slowly to five before touching the hold. The next step is to get into position for the next move. The climber should continue this technique to the top of the wall. Once she has this mastered, put her on a more difficult climb. The goal is to establish the body position completely for efficient movement.

Another version is to place a piece of wrapped candy on a hold. Have the climber climb up to it, take the candy, and unwrap it—all while holding on with the other hand. This makes the climber "lock off" with the holding hand.

Coordination Exercises

BLINDFOLDED CLIMBING

Techniques: hand/foot coordination, memory

Concept: Climbing with a blindfold will help develop an intuitive style of movement. By climbing blindfolded, the climber will be unable to see his hands or feet and therefore will have to remember where he put his hands in order to place his feet. Climbing blindfolded will also teach him to stand on holds he did not think were possible to stand on.

   Activity: Blindfold the climber with a bandana, and have him climb a wall that has quite a few handholds. He should not be able to see any holds. As he progresses in ability with the blindfold on, he can move to a more difficult wall.

Hunter Schumaker wears a blindfold while climbing to develop an instinctive style of movement. Photo: Stewart Green

TENNIS BALLS

Technique: balance

Concept: Some climbers have trouble shifting their weight from side to side without pulling with their arms. This movement should be initiated from the hips and toes to save upper body strength.

Activity: To develop balance, have your student climb with tennis balls in her hands so that she cannot grasp the holds with her hands or fingers. The tennis balls should be used to push and pull against handholds, and she should be using her legs to push up the wall. With the tennis balls, she will shift her weight back and forth so that her legs are doing most of the work. *Some people get pumped doing this exercise because of overgripping the tennis balls.*

Using tennis balls for balance, Kaley Schumaker makes her way up the wall. Photo: Stewart Green

ONE FOOT CLIMBING

Technique: balance

Concept: When a climber loses balance, he will need to compensate with upper body strength to regain balance, wasting valuable energy. The more the student can climb in the balanced position through all moves, the less energy it will take to climb.

   Activity: Use boulder problems (or routes) that are below the climber's maximum onsight ability level. Let the student climb the problem using both feet. Next have the climber do the problem with only the right foot—the left can smear and flag. As he climbs he needs to balance out his body so that he is not swinging or having to adjust to make the moves. He needs to climb the problem at least two or three times with only the right foot, then switch to the left. The more times he climbs the problem, the easier it will get, helping improve his balance with each completion of the problem.

Clipping Techniques

CLIPPING ON THE GROUND

Concept: Clipping can waste valuable energy—especially if clips are fumbled. If you break down clipping positions, only four must be mastered. A climber must be able to clip efficiently with each hand, and each hand must be able to clip a draw facing each direction.

   Activity: You will need an eyebolt to screw into a T-nut in the climbing wall, a quick draw, and a short piece of rope for this exercise. Hang a quick draw, gate opening to the right, from an eyebolt on the wall. The climber will be standing on the ground during this exercise. Using the right hand, have the climber clip the draw, watching the rope until it is in the carabiner and the gate is closed. The clip must be practiced until it is perfect—no fumbling, dropping the rope, or taking more than a count of three to get the rope into the carabiner. The climber must use the same method of clipping the quick draw each time. Once a position is mastered, don't have the climber change her technique; it will be more efficient if the climber doesn't have to think about how to clip a draw. Once the climber has mastered that position with the right hand, turn the quick draw around, gate

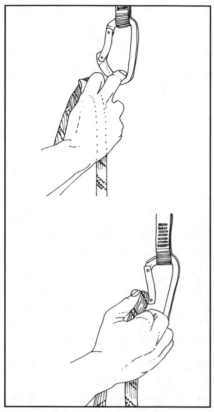

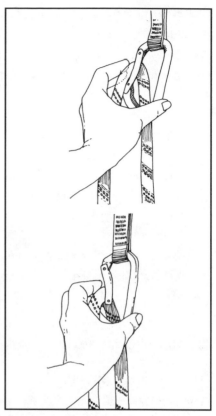

Stabilizing the carabiner with the middle finger of the right hand, the index finger and thumb bring the rope up to the gate and the thumb pushes the rope through.

With the left hand/left gate combination, the climber will stabilize the carabiner with her thumb and middle finger, then push the rope through the gate with her index finger.

opening to the left, and clip it again until mastered, still using only the right hand. Once this is accomplished, the climber can then use the left hand and practice with the quick draw facing each direction.

CLIPPING ON THE WALL

Activity: This is done the same way as the previous exercise, except the climber is on the wall, hanging onto a hold with the right hand while clipping the draw with the left hand. Make sure the climber's position on the wall is relaxed: The arm holding onto the climbing hold is straight, shoulders are relaxed, and the climber is focused on the quick draw. Ideally the climber will reach down for the short piece of rope hanging around her waist, take a deep breath, and then clip the carabiner. Once the climber has done this with each hand, turn the gate of the quick draw the opposite direction and have her practice again with both hands. Make sure the climber is not backclipping or turning the quick draw as she clips in. If the rope is short enough, the climber should be able to just pull it through the carabiner after making each clip instead of having to unclip.

CLIPPING OFF ANYTHING!

Concept: Being able to clip off any hold can be the biggest challenge to a climber moving up the grades. Some climbers may say "Take" right before a clip, rest, and make the clip with no problem. This should tell you, the coach, that the clip is not the problem, the brain is.

Activity: On every route a climber does, do not let him "take" before clipping. His goal should be to make the clip, then say "Take" or continue to climb. Once the climber is at the clipping hold, he should take a deep breath and clip the draw—assuming that it is safe to do so and that the belayer has the proper amount of slack out. Only after the draw is clipped is the climber allowed to say "Take." If the climber is unable to do this, he needs to go down a grade level until he has mastered this technique before advancing to harder climbs. This will create a focus—clip the draw—so that the climber is concentrating solely on the task at hand.

CLIPPING AT WAIST LEVEL

Concept: Pulling up enough rope to clip a quick draw that is over the climber's head creates two problems:

1. The climber must pull up excess rope. This can cause an extra-long fall if the climber doesn't clip the draw, or it can force the climber to put the rope in his mouth in order to pull up enough to clip the quick draw.

2. It makes the climber pull up into a lock off position to reach the quick draw, instead of being in the more comfortable straight-arm position.

Activity: If you have a student who commonly clips above his head, you need to get him to clip the draw closer to waist level to conserve energy. Gradually (over a period of weeks) have the climber clip quick draws only if they are at his head level. After he can comfortably do this, have him clip at shoulder level. Once he has this mastered, work down until he always clips quick draws when they are at his waist level. It is easier to see the draw and put the rope in if a climber doesn't have to pull up excess rope to do it.

Handhold Techniques

SLOPERS, CRIMPERS, GASTONS

Concept: A climber will be better at some holds than others, but it is important to turn weaknesses into strengths.

Activity: The easiest way to work specific holds is using a systems board. A systems board is set up with slopers, crimpers, jugs, gastons, etc. Each type of hold can be worked using different positions of the body—backstep, straight on, etc. Another way to work specific holds is to set up boulder problems or toprope routes with only one type of hold. The key is repetition, and the climber needs to work the weak area over and over again until it becomes a strength.

Chapter 6: **Climbing with the Brain**

"You've already lost if you begin making excuses."

Mental power is typically highly underrated when climbing. Once technique is mastered, 95 percent of climbing becomes mental. If a climber is not prepared to do a climb, or has an excuse, chances are he will not finish the climb. The exercises below will help build up mental power.

Questions to Reduce Pressure

Some climbers put pressure on themselves and begin thinking negative thoughts before even leaving the ground. They may say to themselves, "What if I fall before I get to the last hold?" or "What if I fall at the crux and get last place [in a competition]?" The thought of failure can be self-perpetuating and cause a negative outcome. If a climber is thinking only about falling when he leaves the ground, that is probably going to be the end result of the climb.

Following is one exercise you can do before your student climbs to get rid of the negative thoughts. Pick a climb slightly above his onsight ability level. Have him read his route, then describe the route in his journal. In that description, have him tell you where he will have a problem or possibly fall. If you see negative comments, have him write a "rebuttal" to them. For example: "I will get to the yellow hold; then the clip looks hard." The rebuttal should take the negative out of that comment. "I will get to the yellow hold, take a deep breath, and then make the clip. I can rest on the next blue hold."

Footwork

It takes mental practice to always be aware of where the feet need to be. After awhile the climber will be able to watch her feet and place them precisely. The reaction to look for and place the feet first should come before looking for and placing the hands—something that takes a bit of reversal in the brain to become second nature.

The climber should always be aware of where her feet need to be to *complete* a move. She should place her foot once—watch it the entire way and make sure it is solid—and then concentrate on the rest of the move. Be sure she looks in a 6-foot radius from where she is to see if there are any holds that she might have missed at first glance. If a climber is stuck, have her look down for footholds and move her feet up, instead of trying to stretch too far for the next hold.

Don't Let Go

If the climber is letting go because he is pumped, then he needs to mentally tell his body to relax, shake out, and rest. Have him tell himself to make one more move; it's better to fall making a move than it is to give up and let go. Make sure the climber continues to breathe and create a rhythm for himself.

If he is pumped, he should aim to make one more move—and then one more after that. It is possible to climb *past* a pump. It may feel as though it is impossible to hold on, but the body can go well beyond what the climber believes.

Set Your Position

Each move should be completely finished before starting the next. Have the climber set his hands, feet, and body and be completely balanced before moving again. This will make reaches easier and more stable. Each movement should be controlled, and the climber should always plan on being able to complete the move. If he doesn't think he can do the move, he will probably fail because he will not give it his best effort. Positive attitude can overcome even difficult routes/moves.

One More Move

One way to get your student to push herself is to have her always make—and stick—one more move before she gives up. If you have a climber who is constantly saying "Take," and yet you know she has more moves in her power, do not let the belayer "take" until she tries to make one more move—with effort.

Plan Ahead/Visualize

If the student can see what he needs to do when reading a route, it is almost as though he has done it before and it is easier (part of the body's engrams). Looking at all the moves, he should read the route before stepping onto it, decide which hand needs to be on each hold, where he can rest, and what holds to clip. If he reaches a point in his preview where he does not know what to do, this may be where he will fall or have trouble and use up valuable energy. Can he see the moves after that? Have him work backward from those higher moves to figure out the sequence required to get to that point.

Visualization is a learned skill; it doesn't just happen overnight. Some methods and games (Chapter 12) to learn visualization are "beep," drawing a route from memory then comparing it to the actual route, and closing the eyes to visualize the route.

Your student should do the following things to help improve visualization:

- Relax.

- Go over the route/problem a few times, then close her eyes and visualize it in her mind.

- Include color, shape, and texture of holds when reading a route to help jog the memory.

- Go slowly as she reads.

- Make the moves with the entire body, even though she is standing on the ground.

- Pay attention to the details—make sure small foot- or handholds are not overlooked.

- Have your climber decide how to carry out each section of the climb: fast, slow, carefully, etc.

Block Out the Negative

Encourage your student to take the following steps to help block out negative thoughts:

- If he sees himself falling during the preview of the climb or if it is a difficult sequence, have the student go back and look at the climb again until he can visualize success.

• Before climbing, the student should not decide how far he will go, but he should tell himself "I will succeed" or "I will top out."

• Have him break the climb down into crux sections and easier sections. This will help him to get through the entire climb by relaxing in the easier sections and focusing completely on the harder areas.

• Negative thoughts about the difficulty of a problem can create a negative outcome. By thinking positively, your student is more likely to get farther than he had imagined. He needs to believe that he can do the route/problem.

Have each climber record any negative thoughts in her journal and turn them around. Also have her record anything negative that you heard her say, and have her replace the negative with something constructive that she can use. Although you should help, it's best if the positive and negative phrases come from the student so that they will stick in her mind. For example: "The negative phrase that I used during this practice was 'I am scared to fall.' I replaced that phrase with 'I will practice falling so that it does not scare me so much.'"

Fight the Tendency to Quit While You Are Behind

When a climber finds himself at the back of the pack, either once or often, it is important that he fight the desire to give up before going all out. Make sure you continue to encourage your climber to give it his all, even if he will lose the competition. Any experience fighting—even if the "battle" is lost—will be beneficial in the long run.

Climb for Fun and the Rest Will Follow

Most climbers who are not climbing for fun will sometimes have a difficult time improving their climbing skill level. A climber who is constantly frustrated will be unable to look at the big picture and see where improvement is needed. Make sure your student is motivated by the sport and for herself, and you will find a successful climber. It is refreshing to go to a competition and see the last-place climber with a smile on her face because the routes were good and she had a great time climbing them. As long as a climber is having fun, anxiety should be in the background and not affecting her climbing. This is especially true in competition settings. Positive energy comes from the climbers who are having a good time—whether they are in first or last place.

Engrams

Engrams are the body's muscle memory. The first time a climber goes up the wall, the body is confused as to what motion is needed. The second time the climber goes up the wall, the body starts to understand what is needed for upward motion. The more the student climbs, the easier it gets. This is partly due to engrams. The more a student works a particular move, the easier it becomes. If a climber thinks "I'm going to backstep this move," the body knows what a backstep is and automatically gets into position to perform the move. After awhile it will almost seem as though the climber doesn't have to think about the position; the body will automatically assume the position needed.

The biggest benefit of engrams is the body's ability to remember moves that have been done before. This is the reason it is important for the climber to be versatile and climb all types of routes—to give the body more movement to draw from. If a climber only climbs slabs, then roofs will be difficult and vice versa. If a climber never uses underclings, then that move will not be in his muscle memory, and the moves will be difficult when included on a problem/route. For this reason, it is important for the climber to work his weaknesses more than his strengths.

The biggest downfall to engrams is when movements are learned improperly, the inefficient movement becomes part of the muscles' memory. If a climber always backsteps with her hips facing the wall instead of forming a T with it, she will not be able to use her legs to their full capacity and her backstep will be ineffectual. If a climber always climbs with his arms bent, he won't be able to rest his muscles between moves. Once a bad habit is formed, it takes twice as long to unlearn the habit. If the climber always thinks "I go up to this hold with my right hand" when he actually needs to have his left hand on the hold, it will be difficult to change that pattern because it is ingrained in the engrams. It is cruical to catch climbers' bad habits early on and set them on the right track to moving properly.

Years ago I tried a boulder problem in Estes Park. When reaching for the crux hold with my left hand, I mistakenly reached straight out to a nonexistent hold instead of to the correct edge 2 feet higher. I must have tried the problem ten times that day, each time reaching out to the nonexistent hold. After numerous tries on the problem, I knew exactly where the correct hold was, but my hand would automatically go straight out before going up. Frustrated, I got on the problem and stared right at the correct edge, trying to force my hand to go directly to it. After many more tries, I corrected the bad engram and my fingers landed on the edge without going straight out. A year later, I returned to the boulder problem and did it from the beginning. When I got to the crux, my hand went out to the nonexistent hold before going up. This boulder problem taught me a huge lesson regarding the importance of learning things correctly the first time—and how long it takes the body to "unlearn" something that is done incorrectly.

Falling

One of the most difficult fears of climbing to overcome is the fear of falling. The easiest way to work on this fear is by actually falling—taking short falls over and over again. The climber needs to know that it is not dangerous and that he will not be hurt during a fall. If a climber has had a bad fall and was injured, it can take years to overcome the fear of falling and may take more than just you, the coach, to help overcome that fear. The climber may need to work on mental aspects in general. Taking yoga, Tai-Chi, or other forms of physical and mental exercise help with relaxation and clearing the mind. (Numerous books deal with falling; see the Resources section of the Appendix.)

Falling is an art, but as long as it is done correctly, it is difficult to get hurt, especially on a sport climb. Kevin Gonzales has his hands and feet in front of him to protect him when he hits the rock. Photo: Stewart Green

Chapter 7: **Training Defined**

There are four basic types of training: power, bouldering, power-endurance, endurance. Each type is vital to a well-rounded program, and each needs to be worked on as a separate entity in the training process, one type per training session. Power and bouldering are the most strenuous training on the body. Power-endurance is a little easier, and endurance is the least demanding on the muscular system.

If your student trains two days in a row, the more strenuous type should be worked first. For example, power should be worked the first day and power-endurance or endurance the second day. Or power-endurance should be worked the first day and endurance the second day. Endurance should never be worked first, as the muscles will be fatigued the following day. Work the more difficult training exercises the first day, when the muscles and body are rested and able to perform to their maximum ability.

Each training type is explained in detail in this chapter, followed by four chapters of exercises to use during those particular training days.

Power

Power workouts are typically not very long, as they are very muscularly intensive, but they should involve two to four hours of climbing. Power should be intense, at the climber's maximum strength or above. When you think of a power workout, think of your student doing four to eight hard moves at her limit so that she can't possibly do one more without falling! These moves should be equally hard, or they should get harder with every move on a longer problem. A power problem should not be onsighted, but it should take a few tries and possibly more than a month to complete. If it does not take at least a few tries, it is not "power" but "power-endurance."

- There is no resting on power problems—the moves should be too difficult.

- Power training will teach the student how to do the most physically challenging moves without giving up.

- After a power workout, the climber should have difficulty taking off her shoes—she should be that tired.

- When watching someone work power, you should see her struggle, grunt, and perhaps even shake as she pulls and pushes through moves. If it does not look like she is struggling hard, either she is not trying hard enough (giving up), or she needs a more difficult problem.

Bouldering

Bouldering is becoming its own sport. During practices you will probably just be touching on it with your students. If your gym is set up for bouldering only, be sure to adapt some of the toproping and lead climbing exercises in your practices.

Bouldering on its own is a "power" sport and should be treated as such. While you can have long, endurance-oriented bouldering sessions, bouldering includes hard moves that can be done close to the ground. Bouldering is a great training method to help push climbers beyond what they believe they can do high up a route on a rope. You can also provide assistance (power spot) during moves to help the climber build up the confidence to do difficult moves on his own.

One of the most important things to remember when bouldering is to make sure the area is safe. There should be adequate padding under the problems, no obstacles, and a spotter should be behind every climber. If you are using a regular climbing wall to boulder, make sure you designate and enforce the uppermost bouldering height—no more than 12 to 16 feet.

Power-Endurance (P-E)

A power-endurance (P-E) workout typically consists of three to five hours of climbing. If you have a limited amount of time with your students, you will need to have concentrated P-E workouts. When you think of P-E, think of an intense workout.

After warming up—usually on three to five climbs or boulder problems—have your student begin her power-endurance workout. This consists of the student climbing routes or boulder problems at her ability level for the majority of the workout. If she is climbing routes, she should be leading and pushing her limits on lead—typically either onsighting hard routes or getting on routes that she has to work but can do in two to five tries. If she is bouldering, she should do boulder problems that include twenty to thirty-five moves hard enough that they take more than two attempts to complete.

Power-endurance workouts are shorter training sessions than endurance, but the student should still climb until she cannot climb any longer—three to five hours. Try to have your student get in a minimum of twelve routes with twenty to thirty-five moves close to her onsight level, and at least six above her onsight level.

Below are some samples of activities for power-endurance days:

- Connect shorter, somewhat-difficult boulder problems to make longer power-endurance problems.

- Rock ring "pull-up" workout by Metolius with elastic bands. This workout starts at the top of the rock ring. The climber puts his feet into an elastic band to help with the pull up. Have the climber do twelve repetitions, rest for approximately one minute, and then move to the next hold down. Next have him do ten reps then rest one minute. Keep going down until the climber reaches the hardest hold on the rock ring, and then have him work his way back up—increasing the reps as he gets higher on the rings.

- Pyramid workout. Start on warm-up routes, then gradually work up to more difficult routes. When the student gets to his peak, he should do the same routes in reverse order, forming a pyramid with difficulty. Pick six to ten routes ahead of time so that the student ends up doing twelve to twenty routes during the workout. (See Chapter 13, Pyramids.)

- "Beep." (See description in Chapter 12, Endurance Games and Activities.)

- Negatives. Pull through a move with one arm, then reverse the move slowly, using only one arm at a time. Now do the same move with the other arm. (For more about negatives, see Chapter 9.)

Endurance

This type of training typically involves a long practice session. It is low intensity, and a climber should work to improve movement (technique) during endurance workouts. Because the level of climbing is easier, endurance is the best training workout for concentrating on proper technique. A climber should never feel he is struggling through moves during an endurance workout—unless he is just physically too tired to complete a movement. Endurance will involve longer routes/boulder problems, probably sixty or more hand moves at a time without coming off the wall. Specific ways to work endurance include the following:

- Laps. Have the student climb up and then down-climb routes below his onsight ability level until he falls off. Endurance should be easy, but not so easy that the climber is not benefiting from the workout. If your student has completed several routes without falling (more than five), the route is probably too easy—bump him up a grade. The same goes for only being able to do two laps—bump him down a grade. For maximum benefit he should be able to do three to four laps at a time.

- Add-on. (See description in Chapter 12, Endurance Games and Activities.)

- Clipping. (See description in Chapter 12.)

- Carabiner carry. (See description in Chapter 12.)

- Have the student climb two routes each time he ties in. Climbing the same route twice will build up muscular endurance.

- Make sure the climber takes advantage of rest positions so that he can stay on the wall for a longer period of time. For example, he should stay on the wall for twenty minutes before untying from the rope.

Chapter 8:
Redpointing and Onsighting

Redpointing

The term *redpointing* refers to working out the moves on a route, then climbing the route from the ground up with no falls or hangs. When a climber is just beginning this redpoint tactic, he will want to pick routes very close to his onsight level so that he can learn the techniques involved without becoming too frustrated. Typically the redpoint level should be one number grade above the onsight level, so a climber onsighting 5.12a should be attempting redpoints at the 5.13a level. This does not mean he should skip 5.12b–d; he needs to be working on those as well. As the climber becomes more experienced at redpointing, he should pick climbs that are a grade or two above his onsight abilities.

The reasons for redpointing routes—commonly referred to as "working a route"—are to build up strength, endurance, and power and to increase the mental ability to focus on hard climbs. When working a route, the climber is basically rehearsing so that the body learns the moves before attempting to send the climb. The more often a particular move is worked, the easier it becomes. The more a climber redpoints, the easier it is going to be to read and work out moves. As a route is worked, errors will be eliminated in sequences that could use up valuable energy and strength during a redpoint attempt. Over time, redpointing routes will increase the climber's efficiency and onsight ability.

While working a route, the climber should try to conserve as much energy as possible. This means resting on the rope, using the rope to pull past moves after a fall, and going from bolt to bolt, stopping to rest at each quick draw before continuing on to the next move. Stopping at each bolt on a route gives the climber a chance to rest physically so that he can do each section of moves while fresh and rested. If a move feels too difficult, instead of expending valuable energy, the climber should just pull past the move and come back to it after resting.

The hardest moves should be attempted when the climber is the most recovered or fresh. A good tactic to use on a move that feels impossible is to move to the next hold, put the body into position, and down-climb the sequence. Usually this will help the climber realize where his body needs to be to complete the move. As soon as he is able to do a sequence without falling, he can begin to link sequences together.

Other tactics that can be used are to toprope the climb before leading it, try different sequences, and work the top moves more than the bottom moves. The climber will be more pumped at the top of the climb, so he should have those moves committed to his muscle memory. If he is having trouble with a certain sequence, he can hang on the rope and evaluate the moves before attempting them.

While working a route, the climber also needs to concentrate on efficient clip and rest positions. These techniques should also be committed to memory and made part of the climb.

When the climber feels ready to make his redpoint attempt, he should be sufficiently rested—enough to be fresh and recovered but not so much that the muscles become cold so that he needs to warm up again. Have the climber read the route from the bottom and mentally picture each move. By this time he should have each move and accompanying technique committed to memory. If he is reading the route and can't remember a sequence, he should work that section a little more. Make sure he is mentally prepared; have him put his mind on autopilot, tie in, and go for the redpoint!

Onsighting

The term *onsighting* means to climb a route from the bottom to the top on the first attempt without having prior knowledge of the route. Sometimes climbers use this term even if they have prior knowledge of a climb. Technically, though, this would be a "flash" of the route, not an onsight. Good onsighting requires practice. By climbing on different types of rock, in different gyms, and on unfamiliar routes, climbers will improve their onsight level. A good onsight climber always looks in control and climbs smooth, even when she has never been on the route before. This ability comes from remaining calm, even when faced with awkward clips, difficult crux sections, and unfamiliar sequences.

When choosing a route to onsight, the climber needs to pick a grade that she believes she can climb without taking a fall. Picking a climb that is too difficult will be frustrating for the student, so aim low to start with. Once a few climbs of a certain grade level are mastered, have the student bump up one letter grade at a time. For example, if you have a student who is consistently onsighting 5.10+ in the gym, she can then bump it up to 5.11- or 5.11a. Outside she should try a 5.10, and once she has mastered that grade outside, she can bump up to 5.10+. Remember, all climbs of the same grade are not created equal. If your student isn't able to finish one 5.10+, have her try another that may be more her style.

Onsight climbs typically require more energy than routes that have been climbed previously. The body has not done the moves before, and the climber is on unfamiliar terrain, facing holds that she is not sure about. This can all be mentally draining.

Following are some tips to tell your students about onsighting routes:

- Control your movements—always plan on being able to complete the move.

- Be as efficient as possible with footwork and movement—body tension can be key. Extra moves will expend more energy.

- Your attention must be completely on the task at hand, whether you are concentrating on one move at a time (during a difficult sequence) or taking an overall view (at a rest or during an easier sequence).

- Continue to breathe, and create a rhythm for yourself. Chances are you have actually done the moves before on a different climb, so concentrate on using proper technique that will take advantage of the engrams in your body.

- Create a relaxed atmosphere, an inner calm that you can pull into play while at a rest or during an easier sequence. This will actually help you prepare for the next difficult sequence, even if you are feeling pumped or tired.

- Before tying in for the climb, visualize yourself doing every move—making the clips, resting, and clipping the final anchors. You will have a feeling of success before you have even left the ground, which helps with your positive attitude during the climb.

- Break the climb down into crux and easier sections. This will help you get through the entire climb. If there are only two crux sections and the remainder of the climb is relatively easy, you can relax a little once you get through those difficult sections and concentrate on finishing the climb.

- Have a backup plan if a section you had pegged as "easy" turns out to be a crux. Make the decision to fight through the moves and not give up—or to back off to the last rest and reevaluate the section.

- If you get stuck during your onsight attempt and cannot figure out a sequence, down-climb to a rest and take another look at it. Evaluate where your body was and what hold you need to get to. If it is only three moves, then a large hold, just concentrate on those three moves to get you to the large hold.

- Take the pressure off yourself. Don't believe that if you do not onsight the route that you have failed. Sit down if you fall and analyze why you fell. Find out what you did correctly and praise those things. After a sufficient rest, give it another go as a redpoint.

During onsight competitions, climbers will generally sit in a chair with their back to the wall so that they can't see the climbers ahead of them on the route. This situation can be extremely nerve-racking for some climbers because instead of facing the wall they will be facing the audience.

It's all about the wait—sitting in a chair with her back to the next route, Erin Axtell waits her turn to onsight during a competition. Photo: Craig Axtell

Reading Routes

THE BASICS

It is somewhat difficult to teach someone to read routes, so a laser pointer can come in handy. Bouldering is also a great way to teach route-reading skills, because it is easier to point out the holds on a bouldering wall close to the ground than on a 30-foot climbing wall. The biggest benefit of route reading is creating engrams in the body so that the climber feels as though he has previously completed the moves. Reading a route will help keep the climber on track and locate holds that might be missed while actually climbing the route.

MOVE AROUND

To teach route reading, have the climber stand at the bottom of the wall and walk around to look at the route from different directions. Encourage the climber to move around for a better vantage point from which he can see all the holds on the route. This is especially important on overhanging problems and routes that traverse or wander. Often overlooked when reading a route are the footholds. Make sure the climber reads for both hand- and footholds.

BREAK IT DOWN

One easy way for a climber to read harder routes is to break the climb down into sections. Most climbs do not simply have one hard move after another. Most climbs have easier sections, a crux, an easier section, and then another crux—or an easier section, then a harder section, and then maybe a rest hold. Breaking down the climb into sections can make it easier to climb and less intimidating. This gives the climber the chance to think: If I can make it up to the blue hold, I can shake out, and then tackle the crux. If a 5.11 climber walks up to climb a 5.12a, it can be intimidating. Remind her that not every move on the climb is 5.12a, only some of the moves are. Also keep in mind that a crux to some climbers may not be a crux to others. A crux depends on each individual's strengths and weaknesses.

READ AND MOVE

As the climber reads the route, she should actually enact the movements with her hands and body. While reading a right-hand hold, the right hand should be in the air in the position of the hold. The same is true for body position. If the climber says, "here is my rest," she should drop the resting hand to her side, take a deep breath, and then look for the next hold. Essentially, she should be climbing the route while standing on the ground. Rest holds should prompt a deep breath from the climber. Have your climber relax as she reads on the ground to help her transfer that feeling when on a route.

Ian Spencer-Green, Mike Auldridge, and Tommy Caldwell read the route at the Continental Championship, Vancouver, Canada, 1996. Notice how their hands are synchronized as they determine how to do a move. Photo: Stewart Green

ALTERNATIVES

As the coach, help your student by pointing out alternative moves that could be done. Make sure the climber doesn't get stuck trying a move only one way. There are usually other options, so if one move doesn't work, there may be an alternative. If she gets to a hold that she thinks is a jug and it turns out to be a sloper, she should reanalyze the move or have a backup plan.

READ, READ, READ

The student should read the route as many times as possible before leaving the ground. One time is not enough. Your student should be able to close her eyes and still see the route before ever leaving the ground.

First Read: The first time the climber reads a route, it is to get an overview. Where does the route start? Where does it end? Does it go straight up, traverse, or meander? Locate all the holds for the hands and feet.

Second Read: The second time the climber reads a route, it should be to enact the moves with the entire body.

Third Read: Read rest holds and clipping positions. Work through any crux moves forward and backward so that there is no question on how to do the move.

Final Read: Put it all together. Do the moves on the ground one more time—from the start hold to the final jug, including rests and clips. Envision "topping out."

PROBLEMS

If the climber is having trouble seeing a move, have her go to the next hold up that she is certain of and then backward down the route until she reaches the problem move to find a solution that wasn't obvious. If the climber just cannot read a route and doesn't see it in her head, have her start small. Have her read the first six moves, climb them exactly as she read them, then stop and read the next six moves. Break it down into sections until she is able to read entire routes. Play memory games such as "Beep" (Chapter 12) or "Add on" (Chapter 11).

COMPETITION ROUTES

Climbers competing in onsight competitions usually do not have much time to read a route, so they need to read as efficiently as possible in a short amount of time—usually around five minutes. Sometimes they will have the benefit of other climbers reading the route at the same time, and they can read the route with someone else. Remind your student that competition routes are set to be climbed. Route setters want a climber to get to the top. There won't be "stopper" moves—difficult, but not stopper. There will be minimal rests, so the climber needs to take advantage of any rest, even if it is 5 feet off the ground. Routes usually become more difficult the higher the climber gets, so energy conservation is the ultimate concern in a competition. The climber who arrives at the finishing jug with the most energy will probably do better in the next round or on the next route.

Finding unusual positions on a route is important, but make sure the climber sees things like this stem before leaving the ground. Chris Sharma found this vital stem at a national competition in 1996. Photo: Stewart Green

Make sure the climber checks the following each time he reads a route:

- Footholds

- Handholds

- Clipping positions

- Rest positions

- Holds off to the side that may not be obvious

- Types of holds—underclings, sidepulls, odd moves, etc.

- Odd positions such as toe hooks, stems, or no hand rests

- Ending hold—especially in a competition

- Alternative moves

Chapter 9:
Power Games and Activities

Bump

The object of this game is to teach big moves using momentum and control. You will want to use a boulder problem no longer than eight (big) moves long. Each move should be at the maximum reach/power of the climber you are setting the problem for. Between each hold, find a small, intermediate hold that the climber

In this exercise, the climber will be fully extended when going for the final hold. Set up the problem so that he has to use intermediates to set up his body before making the big move.

can use to get the body established for the "big" move. The intermediate hold should be close to the final hold, but the climber should still have to use some momentum to bump off the intermediate to the final hold. Once the final hold is reached, have the climber bring his second hand up close to set up for the next move. For the first boulder problem, the right arm should be doing the big moves/bumps, then set a second boulder problem going the opposite direction for the other hand. See diagram below for a visual explanation of "Bump."

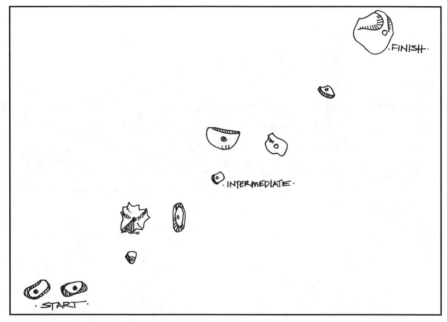

There may be a lot of holds on a bouldering wall, but only pick one that the climber can use as an intermediate between the start hold and finish hold.

Deviation

This game requires two climbers with similar abilities. Set a start and a finish hold. Climber one makes seven moves between the start and finish hold. Climber two climbs the problem, changes two to three of the moves, and climbs it again. The start and finish holds remain constant through the entire exercise. Climber one climbs the problem with climber two's changes, changes two to three of the moves, and climbs again. Each rotation should make the problem slightly differ-ent—possibly harder, possibly easier. The rotations continue approximately ten times. The finished problem will be completely different from what they started with. Designate different start/finish holds, and start the exercise again.

This exercise is great for those climbers who like to set their own boulder problems, and it teaches the climbers movements they may not normally do. It is sometimes useful to pair climbers with totally different climbing styles so that they get a nice variety of moves.

This game can take place during an entire training session, and the students probably will not get bored.

Dynamic Movement

The key here is momentum, using the forces of fluid movement to carry the climber from one position to the next. Dynamic movement does not always mean dynoing—jumping to a hold with no points of contact; often it is simply a matter of generating enough push and pull with the feet and hands so that the body's own weight propels the climber to the next hold. Generally dynamic techniques are used only when the next hold is farther than the climber can reach from a locked-off position or when the footholds are too low, forcing the climber to smear high and use a dynamic move to get to the next hold.

In addition to momentum, dynamic movement requires excellent timing to be useful. Timing means knowing at what point pull turns to push and when to let go of a lower hold so that the hand reaches the next hold at the deadpoint— when the climber is going neither up nor down—of the movement. If she lets go too early, she won't have enough momentum, or her momentum might actually throw her away from the wall. If she lets go too late, she will either miss the hold altogether or catch it as she is falling back down, thus shock-loading her hands and making the move less efficient. If the timing is right, the movement should smoothly propel the climber toward the next hold so that she can grab it at the deadpoint and catch hold of it with minimal effort.

Finger Board Workouts

Working out on a finger board will develop muscular endurance. The climber can use a finger board to hang on holds, move between holds, use each hold for a certain length of time before moving to another hold, or do pull-ups to develop lock off strength. Finger boards typically have everything from good jugs to nearly impossible crimps/slopers. Therabands can be hung from the bottom of the board to help take some of the climber's weight off the hands. Beware of overtraining on finger boards, as tendonitis can develop easily with such a concentrated workout.

There are a lot of options available for training on a finger board.
Photo: Stewart Green

Systems Training

This is one of my favorite training tools! A systems training board is an integral part of any good climbing gym and involves repetitive motion with each side of the body. A systems wall typically consists of at least eight "system tiles" with a variety of grips—slopers, pinches, jugs, and pockets—in a definite pattern, which are approximately 1½ feet apart, offset approximately 1 foot. A systems wall does not have to incorporate systems tiles but can use regular holds set in a pattern so that moves can be duplicated equally with each side of the body.

SYSTEMS BOARD MODEL

The systems board at the ROCK'n & JAM'n gym (see photo) is an example of how to set up your own systems board; it includes a lot of handholds and footholds for variety. The systems board should overhang at least 15 degrees, but the ideal angle is between 20 and 35 degrees. The height should be at least 12 feet. An ideal systems board has adjustable angles. Positions can be mastered at one angle, so adjusting to a steeper angle will make it more challenging. Notice the small footholds on the bottom of this wall and the symmetrical climbing holds on the remainder of the wall. More information on building systems walls can be obtained from the manufacturers of systems tiles, such as Pusher out of Salt Lake City, Utah. In my opinion Pusher is the best, but you can also check out Nicros and Franklin.

This systems board shows a nice angle, approximately 15 degrees, with a thick pad underneath.
Photo: Stewart Green

BODY BALANCE

The main goal of systems training is to develop equal strength on both sides of the body. You want your climbers to do the same movement on each side so that they do not have glaring weaknesses on one side. If you find that one side is not as strong as the other, have the climber do more repetitions on the weak side to bring it up to equal strength.

CONTROL

The climber should do every movement with control, even when tired. If movements become sloppy, have the climber use larger, easier holds so that technique does not suffer. Feet should almost always be on the board, and the legs should be used to "push" through the moves. You or another climber can help the climber through moves by "power spotting" or taking weight off of the climber as he pushes through a move. The important thing is to complete the move *properly*, not just complete it.

WEAKNESSES TO STRENGTHS

One of the best things about systems training is that it works weaknesses in a controlled environment. If the student is horrible with slopers, he can use the best slopers on the wall and then advance to worse slopers as his ability improves.

ALL-AROUND PERFORMANCE

Make sure the climber is concentrating on all aspects of climbing as he is doing the movements (remember engrams). If a climber is just thinking about the upper body and letting the feet slide around on the wall, he will develop bad habits as he develops strength. A climber should be careful with the feet and use quiet feet, placing them firmly, yet delicately, always conscience of all aspects of his climbing performance.

FAILURE

All systems board exercises can be done to "failure," which is an important notion. If a climber doesn't know how far he can push his body, he will not be able to push to the point of failure. When doing reps on the different exercises, try to get the climber to go to the point of falling at least a few times during the session, especially on "holding" exercises. Once a climber knows his point of failure, he will be able to push himself farther on routes. Again, make sure the integrity of the exercise remains constant, even at the point of failure.

"IT'S TOO EASY."

Once the climber feels he is no longer benefiting from a systems workout, you can up the ante and have him climb with worse footholds. This will work his body tension and core strength. With a good systems wall, the angle can be made steeper, making the exercises more difficult without changing the holds. The student can always use worse handholds to make the workout more challenging. Have the climber train with weights on a belt around the ankles or wrists. It doesn't take much; one- to five-pound weights are sufficient.

Remember the following when working with students on the systems board:

- Watch for imbalance. If a weakness is found on one side, have your climber do double the exercises on the weak side to create a "balance" in the body movements.

- Train to the point of failure. Failure is the point at which the fingers absolutely cannot hold on any longer.

- Always use a spotter.

- Let the spotter take some of the weight off the climber (power spot) so that the repetitions can be completed.

- Train with different partners to experiment with different exercises.

- Work weaknesses!

- Set goals for each workout and stick it out, even when close to failure.

- Keep track of the workouts so that you can see improvements over time.

- Refine the exercises so that they are completed to perfection.

- Repetition is important.

- Focus on each movement and isolation exercise.

- Use relatively good holds if necessary so that the purpose of the exercise is not compromised. If you're working body tension, the fingers shouldn't be the body part to fail.

Some exercises are listed below, along with a sample systems board workout. Be sure to do all the exercises on a variety of holds—slopers, pinches, pockets, etc.—to develop a range of "strengths" in the body.

- **Lock offs 1:** Lock off on the right arm to raise the body upward. The climber reaches as high as possible to the left, right, or straight up but does not actually weight or grab the next hold. When you reach up, hold the position, then lower back down to the starting position. Now he rises up again, holds the position, and then lowers back down to the starting position. Have him do three (or more) lock offs on each arm before moving to the next arm.

Seth Lytton works his lock off strength on a systems board. Photo: Stewart Green

- **Lock offs 2:** Another way to develop lock off strength is to go from one hold to the next, but instead of grabbing the hold immediately, hold the position, count to five, then grab the hold and repeat with the other arm. The climber continues all the way up the systems board or completes at least three lock offs per arm.

- **Body tension:** To develop body tension, the climber grasps a hold in each hand with the arms straight and releases the feet. The feet should swing away, but the climber should try to fight it. Now she puts the feet back on the wall on higher holds, moves the hands up to the next holds, and repeats. This exercise can also be done with one foot at a time. For example, the left foot would be hanging free, and the right foot would be on a hold. The climber releases the right foot, fights the swing, and replaces the right foot higher up. Then she repeats the series with the left foot.

- **Pulse:** A pulse involves holding on to a hold with one hand and reaching for the next hold with the other hand. Instead of grabbing the hold, the climber returns to the original position, and then reaches again in a pumping motion. On the third reach she actually grabs the hold. The movement should be controlled up and back down again, but the hold is not touched and weighted until the final reach. The hold should be at her maximum extension so that it is a struggle to get to the hold on the third reach.

- **Straight on:** When practicing exercises facing the wall (not backstepping), the climber should concentrate on using the leg to "rock over" toward the handhold. I like to do straight-on exercises with the following hand positions: gaston, the palm of the hand facing away from the body; pinches, an open-handed grip; and slopers, an open-handed grip that is better when the body weight is low.

To avoid using too much upper body strength, Seth pulls with the toe, rocking his hips over his left foot. Photo: Stewart Green

• **Backstep:** Again, this move involves using the *outside edge* of the climbing shoe, with the side of the hip close to the wall. The easiest way to determine which way to use the backstep is to decide which hand you need to be reaching with. If reaching with the right hand, the right hip should be against the wall, and the right outside edge should be on a foothold.

Using the systems board, Seth practices backstepping with his right hip against the wall and reaching up with his right hand. Photo: Stewart Green

Sample System Board Workout

Instructions for this sample workout:

Hold: The type of hold that should be held in the hand. Because holds vary, this list is not comprehensive. If a climber needs to work "slopers," then do each exercise on slopers. If a climber needs to work pockets, use only pockets.

Movement: The body position for the movement to be performed.

Lead: Which hand/foot should start the movement. "Alternating" refers to switching hands with each movement. Most exercises that are referenced as alternating can be done so that the climber goes all the way up the wall with the right hand leading, returns to the ground, and then leads with the left hand.

Repetitions: Each movement should be repeated a minimum of five times on each hand. As a climber progresses with systems training, she should be able to increase the number of repetitions or use worse holds.

This particular sample workout focuses on a variety of techniques and is designed for the climber to complete from beginning to end in one session. When designing workouts specifically for your students, you can set up an entire systems board workout to work a specific hold, such as slopers. After using the workout below a few times, you will know how many laps your student is able to do, and you will be able to design workouts specifically for that student.

Lap 1	Hold	Large jug
	Movement	Backstep
	Lead	Start with the right hand to the top of the board, come down, and then switch to the left. Stay in the backstep position the whole way up. Watch that the right hip is against the wall—the pelvis should be perpendicular to the wall.
Lap 2	Hold	Medium crimper on system tile
	Movement	Straight on/lock off, continue up the board
	Lead	Start with right hand to the top of the board, lock off on each movement; come down and then switch to left hand.
Lap 3	Hold	Large crimper
	Movement	Backstep and lock off. Hold for three to five seconds. Grab the hold, then backstep and lock off for the next hold.
	Lead	Alternating

Lap 4	Hold	Good crimper
	Movement	Abs. Straight on, move right hand up, and then right foot.
	Lead	Climb with only one foot on (rt.), let the body come away from the wall, then replace the right foot on the next hold up. Go to the top of the wall, come down, rest, and then switch to left hand/foot lead.
Lap 5	Hold	Slopers
	Movement	Straight on
	Lead	Lead with the right hand. Go from one sloper to the next moving the feet up as you go. Right hand moves up, left hand follows, then right leads again to the top of the wall. After reaching the top, come down and switch to lead left.
Lap 6	Hold	Sidepull
	Movement	Backstep, pulsing three times, then grab the hold on the third pulse and move to the next position.
	Lead	Right hand reaches, right hip is against the wall. After reaching the top, come down, rest a minute, and then switch to the left lead (hip and hand).
Lap 7	Hold	Crimper/sloper (or both, alternating them)
	Movement	Straight on. Rock over the lead foot. Hold each position for three to five seconds before grabbing the hold. Lock off with the left hand, reach with the right, pause for three to five seconds, grab the hold, and repeat with the right hand locking off with the left hand reaching.
	Lead	Alternate hands
Lap 8	Hold	Gaston (palm out)
	Movement	Straight on. Move feet up and then reach up into the gaston. (Holds should be pretty wide apart so that the gaston movement can be felt in its entirety.)
	Lead	Alternating

Lap 9	Hold	Undercling
	Movement	Straight on. Move feet high, then reach up into the next undercling.
	Lead	Right hand leads, then left comes up. Right continues to lead to each hold. After reaching the top, come down and go up again with a left lead.
Lap 10	Hold	Medium crimper or large sloper
	Movement	Abs. To work the core of the body, start with hands on one or two large holds. Arms are straight, and the knees are slightly bent so that the feet start at knee level and walk down the wall on holds toward the floor. At the farthest point—the toes of the shoe are extended and the body is now straight, with the arms completely extended—the climber releases the core body tension (abs), and lets the lower body come away from the wall so that the body is now hanging dead vertical from the hands. To work the abs, pull one foot back onto the wall, reaching and sticking it to the last foothold that was touched. Release the core again and bring the opposite foot to the same hold. Bring the feet up to knee level and repeat. Walking the feet down the wall changes the body position slightly each time so that when the core is extended—stretched to the maximum—it should be very difficult to bring the foot back onto the wall and stick the hold.
	Lead	Alternate. Start with feet at knee level and walk them down the wall.

Campus Board Workouts

One of the quickest ways to increase a climber's contact strength is by campusing. A campus board is a series of wooden strips placed at intervals on an overhanging wall. A campus board can be set up so that it alternates one good rung and one

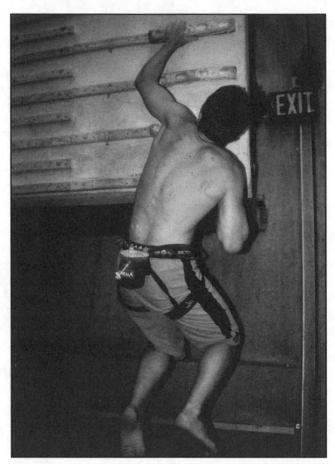

At the U.S. Climbing Team Junior Pro Camp, Josh Spear cranks on the Boulder Rock Club campus board. Photo: Rod Willard

bad or so that an entire row is one size rung and the next row up is another size. Another way to build a campus board is to have each vertical row be the same size.

Feet are not allowed on a campus board, so all movements are done with the upper body. The body should remain still during the movements, without a lot of swinging (momentum) from side to side. To start a campus workout, the climber should use the largest rungs available and try to go from one rung to the next with the arms. Basically, one arm locks off and the other arm reaches. The next step is to skip rungs. For example, the climber goes from rung one to rung three with the right hand, matches with the left hand, and then goes from rung three to five with the right hand and so on. The climber can repeat the exercise leading with the other arm. I will not go into other specific workouts because a lot of information is available in training books with greater detail (see the Resources section of the Appendix).

Campus board workouts can be damaging to young climbers' tendons if overused, but a lot of strength can be developed quickly from this type of workout.

Campus board workouts are a complete training session. Do not let your students use the campus board after a long practice—it is not a "cool down" tool. If you have a student campusing to increase contact strength—the strength of the fingers on immediate contact with a hold—he should warm up for a minimum of thirty to forty-five minutes before even attempting to campus. The campus board workout should then be a maximum of 30 minutes. If your student wants to climb easy routes after the workout, that is fine, but it should only be warm-up level routes to work the overall body muscles.

Negatives

One of the best ways to increase upper body strength is through negatives. This is to be done in a bouldering area or on a systems wall. Choose one good hold, and have the climber grab the hold with her right hand. Now have the climber reach as far up the wall as possible with the left hand. She can either be straight on the wall or backstepped. When the climber has reached as far as possible, have her lower down slowly to the starting position. Count to three as she comes down so that she is lowering her body slowly, not quickly dropping. This exercise should be spotted so that if the climber is unable to get all the way up or needs help coming down slowly she can be power spotted. Have the student complete three to five negatives, then repeat this exercise on the other hand. Remember, the point of the exercise is to lower the body slowly and work against gravity.

Vary this exercise by using different starting holds (slopers, pinches, crimps, etc.) or by having the climber reach in different directions (straight up, slightly forward, slightly back).

Chapter 10:
Bouldering Games and Activities

Many of the games in Chapter 9, Power Games and Activities, are the same for bouldering, because bouldering equals power. Games used for power can be done either on a rope or on a bouldering wall and are meant to be rather short. Power moves are usually less than a series of eight difficult consecutive moves.

Categoric Cling

For this game, write the names of different types of holds (sloper, crimper, jug, side pull, undercling, etc.) on individual pieces of paper and drop them into a hat. Have your climber reach into the hat and draw out a slip of paper. Whatever type of hold drawn is the type of boulder problem she will need to complete. If there are boulder problems set up using only one type of hold, you can just use these problems. If there are no preset problems that use only slopers, for instance, have the climber traverse the wall using only slopers. Once the climber has completed the problem or traverse in both directions to your satisfaction, or for a set amount of time, she can draw another type of hold and the game continues.

Team Comp

This game can be played if you are instructing many individual students and you want to get them together for a training session.

Start by dividing the climbers up into an even number of teams. For example, if you have twelve climbers, make four teams of three climbers or three teams of four climbers. Form the groups evenly so that each group has advanced, intermediate, and beginner climbers. Once you have your teams, each climber makes up and sets one or two boulder problems. You can determine a maximum number of moves or leave it open to the climbers. Once all of the problems are set, have each climber show the rest of the climbers his problem. After all the problems have been explained or sample-climbed by the setter, start the clock.

Give each climber a piece of duct tape. After completing a problem, each student will come to you for a mark on her tape. Give the climbers approximately one hour to do as many problems as they can. Encourage them to work in their teams, because the problems completed are tabulated for each team. Ideally, the climbers should be going from problem to problem as a group and completing the problems together. This will help the beginner climbers understand how to do harder problems and will encourage the better climbers to help the beginners—improving everyone's skills in the process.

At the end of the designated time, tabulate the scores by combining the number of problems completed by each team. The team with the most points wins. *(Thanks to Zoe Kozub and Seth Mason for sharing this game at a Junior Pro Camp.)*

Bouldering Competition

For an informal bouldering competition, the problems can be set by the climbers, by the route setters, or by you. It is best to have a mixture. Again, you will need several climbers for this type of competition. However, you can do the competition with one climber to get her used to "competing."

When the climbers make up problems, they must set problems that they can climb but may be difficult for other climbers. The biggest problem with bouldering comps is having them adequate for the range of climbers at the session. You can set the competition so that the better climbers are not allowed to climb certain problems, and the beginner climbers are not allowed to try the hardest problems. Scoring can be done in a number of ways. Either list the climbs by difficulty and give each one an assigned point value or score the competition based on the number of climbs completed. Give the climbers a set amount of time to complete as many problems as possible.

These informal competitions are nice to have before a bouldering competition to get your students into the practice of deciding strategy—and to build their confidence.

Bouldering Pyramids

HOUR GLASS

A bouldering "hour glass" should take an entire workout to complete. If the climber finds it is too easy, and he is not falling—especially toward the middle of the workout—then the problems need to be more difficult. The hour glass workout requires six boulder problems. The first three problems are relatively easy. The climber should be able to complete them with a maximum of one fall. The student climbs the first three problems three times each—climbs problem one three times, moves on to problem two, climbs it three times, and so on. Moving on to the next level, there are two harder problems, which the climber will complete within four attempts. At the next level, there is only one problem that the climber will complete one time. This problem should take the climber at least four tries to complete; if it takes less time the problem is too easy. Once the sixth and hardest problem is completed, the climber goes back to problem five and does it two more times, then problem four, and so on. Then the climber moves on to problems one through three, again climbing each problem three times.

HOUR GLASS EXAMPLE:

Problem 1 (easy)   **Problem 2 (easy)**   **Problem 3 (harder)**
3 times   3 times   3 times

Problem 4 (difficult)   **Problem 5 (more difficult)**
2 times   2 times

Problem 6 (extremely difficult)
1 time

Problem 5   **Problem 4**
2 times   2 times

Problem 3   **Problem 2**   **Problem 1**
3 times   3 times   3 times

BOULDERING PYRAMID

This pyramid workout includes ten boulder problems. The problems steadily build from the easiest to the hardest, and then the climber works back down from the hardest to the easiest. Problem one is the easiest; problem ten is the most difficult. Climbers should be able to onsight problems one through three. Problems four to six should be more difficult, taking the climber at least two to three tries to complete. Problems seven through ten should continue to increase in difficulty. Problem ten may not be completed but should be worked until it is nearly sent. The "Bouldering Pyramid" is similar to the "Hour Glass" but it has more problems and less repetition per problem. There are a total of nineteen stages in the Bouldering Pyramid and twenty-seven total completions in the Hour Glass.

BOULDERING PYRAMID EXAMPLE:

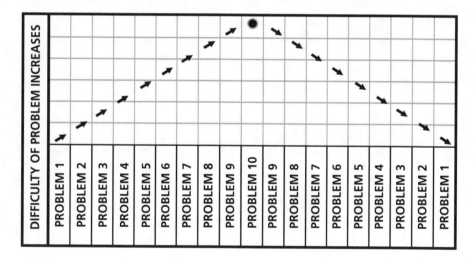

Chapter 11: **Power-Endurance Games and Activities**

Add On

There are many ways to play this game; below are two of the basics. Have fun with this game and try to make up your own variations to keep it interesting. The moves should be difficult, as this is power-endurance training. To play you will need at least two climbers.

- **Version One:** The first climber does three to four moves, and then the second climber does the same number of moves. The first climber repeats his moves, the second climber's moves, and adds on the same number of moves. The climbers rotate so that each person does all the moves sequentially. Each time, the climbers start at the beginning of the problem and do all the moves. This exercise is great for building endurance and memorization, and the moves should be difficult enough so that one climber eventually falls.

- **Version Two:** Each climber does eight to twelve moves. The second climber then does the first climber's moves and adds on the same number of moves. On the first climber's second turn, she starts with the second climber's moves and then adds on the same number. Each climber does sixteen to twenty-four moves at a time with this variation. These moves should be more difficult and work power-endurance. By doing more moves and less repetition, the climbers are working more onsight skills than engram building.

Bad Holds!

This exercise is great if you have a climber who enjoys making up her own problems, or you can make up the problem. On a bouldering wall have the climber make up a problem with at least twenty-five moves but no more than thirty-five. The problem should be challenging, as it is power-endurance. Have the student climb the problem once. Now take the three best holds on the route and replace them with holds in the vicinity that are now the worst holds on the route. Use holds that are available on the wall; you won't be physically moving any holds for this exercise. Have the climber do the problem again, and take the next three best holds on the route and make them the worst holds. Continue until the climber either falls or the route is just too difficult, then move on to another problem, continuing the exercise.

4x5

The name of this exercise refers to doing four problems in five minutes. Set four relatively difficult boulder problems. The climber does one problem as many times as possible in five minutes, aiming for a minimum of four times. After the five minutes, the climber can rest for five minutes, then move on to the next problem. If the climber falls on the problem, he gets back on where he fell off. He must do every move on the problem a minimum of four times.

4x4's

- **Version One:** This works best when you follow the climber around, coaching, encouraging, and nagging. Designate four boulder problems (twelve or fewer moves) that are at the students climbing limit. The student should be able to complete each problem the first time through, doing all the problems back-to-back, with no rest in between. The basis for "4x4's" is that your student does each problem four times, but only one lap on *each* problem, before going back to problem number one and starting over again. The climber should literally be running between problems and trying to climb them as fast as possible. Time her because the amount of time taken to climb the first round is the amount of time she is allowed to rest before starting the next round—a maximum of two minutes' rest between rounds. Each round is done as quickly as possible.

- **Version Two:** For a variation on "4x4's" she can do the first round as quickly as possible, take a two-minute rest, and then climb the second round as slowly as possible—locking off each move without grabbing the next hold.

Round three should be quick again, and round four should be slow. You need to be the cheerleader—urging her to climb as quickly as possible on rounds one and three, and power spotting as needed so that she can get through the problems each time.

Home Base

For this exercise, you pick a "start" hold on a bouldering wall. Make sure you pick a hold that is surrounded by a variety of holds so that the climber has plenty of directions in which to go. The start hold should be good enough to rest and recover on. Have the climber begin climbing away from the start hold for about six to eight moves, using any holds he wants. As soon as you say "stop" the climber retraces the same moves back as fast as possible to the start hold. Now the climber is allowed to rest on the hold until you tell him to go again. This time, the climber is not allowed to use any of the holds that he used on his first "lap." Repeat this at least three to four times from "home," and then pick another start hold.

No Shake, No Take

No Shake, No Take is a great power-endurance game. It involves finding a route at the climber's limit that she can climb when fresh at the beginning of practice. It should be a climb without a definitive crux. On the climb, she is not allowed to shake out on any holds or say "take" at any time; she must do the moves or fall trying. At the end of a practice, have her climb the route again, three times on lead or toprope, or varying the two. On the first climb, when she falls, have her come down and rest for one minute. Have her climb the route again, come down when she falls, rest one minute, and then climb the route one last time. Each time she will probably not get as high on the route, but she should keep pushing herself, trying to get as far as possible. If she is completing the route each time, it is too easy, and she should bump it up a grade!

Numbers Game

A fun way to diversify a bouldering session is to play the Numbers game. Write the numbers "3" through "10" on individual pieces of paper and drop them in a hat.

Have a climber draw out a number. Each number represents the number of holds and problems that climber will make up. If your student draws out the number "5," he will make up five boulder problems that are five moves long. Each move should be difficult to complete.

If you have more than one student in a session, the Numbers game can turn into a session of Add On. If one climber draws out the number "3" and the other climber draws out the number "7," that is the number of moves each climber must add on to the problem.

Pacing

Pacing is extremely important when a climber is on a route so that they continue a consistent pace the whole way, especially if it is a route without a crux. Pacing will change if there is a crux. The basic concept of pacing is to keep a steady pace with both the hands and feet throughout an entire climb.

After the climber is warmed up on holds of her choice, you should begin to pick holds you want the student to use, sometimes varying the difficulty slightly so that the climber does easy and difficult moves at the same pace. During the more difficult problems, have your student doing approximately twenty to thirty hard hand moves.

As the climber begins the problem, you will count along with each foot and hand movement (1 . . . 2 . . . 3 . . . 4 . . . 5 . . . 6, etc.) setting the pace for the climber. Start off counting relatively slowly so that the climber can get used to whatever pace you have set. As the climber advances with this exercise, you can quicken the pace.

The main advantage of this exercise is to get the climber used to climbing at something other than the pace he normally climbs at—all climbers need variety in their pacing.

Pacing with Rests

This is the same exercise as above, except that you give the climber set amounts of time to rest. As you count, you will say "rest" or "stop" at various times and have the climber shake and rest completely, waiting for your command to continue climbing. This will help a climber who is reluctant to rest. Make sure the climber is using proper rest positions while "stopped" on the problem. I usually give my students around three rest points—usually in a place they can rest both hands at once—during a twenty-to-thirty-move problem. Have the climber stay in the rest position until she has shaken out each hand three times and taken at least three deep breaths.

Stick

This exercise will develop quick thinking and help with onsight ability. Your student will be bouldering, and you will have a pointer stick. Use the stick to point to holds for the climber. The pointer will also tell the climber which hand to use to grab a hold. The climber will need to find correct body and rest positions, and he needs to try to stay on the wall as long as possible. You can count the number of moves, trying to get at least twenty hard moves in on each game.

Stick 2

This game will help a little more with the student's endurance and thinking through body positions for unexpected moves. Pick a start and end hold on a bouldering wall that will take approximately twenty moves to traverse. You will pick all the holds along the way for the climber's right hand. The climber can pick the holds for the left hand. Begin on the start hold and pick the first right handhold. The climber can now pick the left. After the climber has chosen the left hold, you pick the next right hold. Continue on until he reaches the end hold. For the second lap, have the climber start at the beginning hold once again. This time you pick the left handholds and the climber chooses the right handholds. Do at least four to six laps, and you can go on different walls, in different directions, etc. This exercise is great for climbers who like to make up their own problems, but with a variation. If the climber continuously chooses holds that are too big, you can have her make large moves to small holds or awkward moves that make the jug a less-positive option.

This is a power-endurance workout, so the moves should be difficult but doable and push the climber. If the moves are not difficult enough, the climber will not be getting enough out of the workout.

Chapter 12:
Endurance Games and Activities

"Beep"

This game works memorization, an important tool to have during onsighting and redpointing. You, the coach, make up a boulder problem approximately twenty to thirty moves long but relatively easy for the climber. You then point out the problem, which should not be marked—one time only—to the climber. The climber then tries to climb the problem from memory. If the climber touches or uses an incorrect hold, you say "Beep" and point out the correct hold. The climber must go back one hold and continue on the problem without touching the floor. The second time the climber is "beeped," he must go back two moves and then continue again, three moves backward for the third beep, etc. The climber must stay on the wall until the entire problem has been completed.

After this exercise is performed a couple of times, the climber will be much better at remembering holds and will probably be able to do it with no beeps. Once a climber has mastered the game, add feet to the memorization to make it more difficult. This is an excellent exercise for a climber who is unable to read routes very well.

Breath with Every Clip

Some climbers do not breathe or relax when they are on the wall. Sometimes clipping a quick draw can be the crux of a climb and the student may hold her breath until after the clip is made. In order to help the climber relax before each clip, she should practice this exercise.

Each time the climber gets to a clip, she needs to get situated into an ideal clipping position. Before picking up the rope to clip, she should look at the ground, inhale deeply, and then exhale. This will create a relaxed stance and the climber can now pick up the rope and clip without being tense. Have her practice this on every clip—a big deep breath, and then clip. Closing her eyes during the breath can help her relax even more.

Carabiner Carry

This is ultimate relay game for a single climber. Use a long bouldering wall that is relatively steep and at least 20 feet long. At one end of the wall, hang ten carabiners from an eyebolt or bolt hanger. At the other end of the wall, hang one bolt

Carabiner carry: On one end of the wall, set up ten carabiners hanging from an eyebolt. The climber must start at the other end of the wall, traverse down for one carabiner at a time, and then traverse back. All the carabiners must be moved before the climber steps off the wall. Photo: Stewart Green

hanger or eyebolt. Starting at the end of the wall with the one empty bolt hanger, have the climber traverse down the wall to the carabiners at the other end. The climber then picks up one carabiner, attaches it to his harness or chalk bag belt, and then traverses back to the other end. Hooking the first carabiner on the bolt hanger, the climber now goes back for the second carabiner and continues until all the carabiners have been moved from one end of the wall to the other. The climber can rest whenever possible on the wall but should not be allowed to step down off the wall to rest. This exercise works best with a partner who can follow the climber, encouraging him to complete each lap on the wall. It can be very frustrating for the climber, but it will help to build incredible endurance. This exercise will take approximately twenty to thirty minutes to complete and can be repeated to decrease the time spent on the wall. This exercise will also teach the climber to move efficiently in order to save energy.

Circuit Bouldering

Use a very easy circular boulder problem approximately ten to fifteen moves long that starts and ends on the same hold, and is set up to do continuous laps without stopping. The climber should try to do as many laps as possible—five to ten—with the goal of becoming a more fluid climber. Your climber should do each move without pausing on the holds—developing a rhythm. This exercise takes a lot of practice but will pay off in endurance and form (fluidity). The body should do the moves so that the climber doesn't have to think about the moves and the body is doing them instinctively. If the problem is set well, the climber should be able to climb it backward for variety. If this is the case, the climber needs to complete at least five laps going in one direction before switching.

Clipping

To become more efficient at clipping, the climber should always watch the quick draw from the time he decides to begin the clip until the rope is secure in the carabiner. If his eyes are taken off the draw, valuable energy will be wasted making the clip if it is not done correctly the first time, because he will have to reposition the rope.

Set up quick draws 6 to 8 feet apart on a long bouldering traverse so that the climber is no more than 10 feet off the ground, and tie a short (15-foot) rope around the climber's waist. Have the student traverse back and forth, concentrating on clipping the draws. There are only four possible clipping positions—left hand, right hand, and the draws facing right or left (see Chapter 5 for clipping positions). Be sure he practices all four positions. You will notice that most climbers have at least one weak clipping position, so make sure they concentrate on becoming efficient with each position.

A few important things to remind your climber of when clipping:

- Beware of back clipping when putting the rope into the carabiner

- Watch body position when clipping. The rope should always be in front of the body, never running behind the leg.

Instructor Michelle Hurni demonstrates watching the quick draw while making a clip on a steep wall at Boulder Rock Club. Photo: Rod Willard

- Never put the rope in the mouth to pull up more rope for clipping. A climber who needs more rope should reach farther down the rope before pulling it up. Having the rope in the climber's mouth puts him in danger of losing teeth in the event of a fall.

- Make sure the climber watches the quick draw from the time he starts the clip until the rope is secure in the bottom carabiner of the quick draw.

Elimination

Start with a section of a climbing wall that is at least 20 feet across. Pick a start hold on one end of the wall and a finishing hold on the other end. Have your student traverse the wall, using whichever holds she wants. From here there are two versions of this game:

- **Version One:** The coach eliminates one to three holds that the climber used to get across the wall. These holds are now off limits, so mark them with a piece of chalk or tape. The climber traverses the wall again, using whichever holds she wants, except the eliminated holds. Now eliminate one to three holds from that traverse. This game continues until there are very few holds left that have not been eliminated. You should eliminate holds, so that the wall gets more difficult with each traverse.

- **Version Two:** The climber chooses which holds to eliminate from the holds he used in the traverse. Because this will typically produce an easier end result, this method should be used while warming up.

Follow the Leader

This is a bouldering game in which one climber "leads" and the other follows. There are two ways to play this game.

- **Version One** (also called "Tied Together Clipping"): Place eyebolts in bolt holes on the wall approximately 5 to 7 feet apart. Hang a quick draw on each eyebolt. Two climbers are attached by approximately 7 to 10 feet of slack rope between them. This works well on a large boulder where they can traverse at least 25 feet, but preferably more.

  The climber leading gets on the wall and makes the first and second clip. The climber following gets on the wall. There must be one draw clipped

While tied together, these two students boulder around this freestanding boulder while the "leader" clips the draws and the "second" unclips. A great endurance building exercise! One draw is always clipped between the climbers.
Photo: Stewart Green

between the climbers at all times. When the following climber gets to draw one, she unclips the draw. The lead climber must now clip draw three before the follower can unclip draw two. Once they reach the end of the wall, they should rest and then switch positions.

The climbers are not allowed to step off the wall. This will teach them to rest whenever possible—especially when the other climber is clipping/unclipping. They must work together so that each clip can be clipped and unclipped (while still having one draw clipped). At no time can both draws be unclipped simultaneously.

- **Version Two:** In this version, the leader will do a series of movements, with the second climber following the movements exactly. The climbers must stay close together, so that the second climber can see what moves the first climber is completing.

Hold Position (Four Count)

Some climbers tend to climb very fast, getting out of balance during each move. Sometimes they sway and have to adjust to rebalance, which can make a climber's movements look "jerky."

Have the climber get on a route that is moderately difficult. Each time the climber reaches for a handhold, she must get into the perfect position to hold it for a count of four. Her hand is not allowed to touch the next hold until she has held the position and counted to four. At this point, she can grab the next hold and move her feet. She must follow this procedure the entire way up the route, counting to four before actually touching the next hold.

Horse Race

This wonderful game can last a few hours. You will need to make a chart for this activity that lists all the climbers' names, and give each of them a starting point. To get out of the starting gate, climbers must complete three warm-up climbs below their onsight level, which will vary by individual climber (see chart for examples.)

Once the climbers are out of the starting gate, they must begin to onsight and redpoint climbs. In order to move ahead in the race, they need to progress to climbs of the same or higher grade without falling. Once they have completed a climb at a certain level (say 5.11), they are not allowed to go backward (to 5.11-, for example) to move ahead. If they climb routes of a lesser grade, they do not get points for that climb. They must continue to climb equal or harder climbs to advance in the game.

The beauty of this game is that it puts everyone on an even level, and climbers of all abilities can compete against one another. The climber to complete the chart first is the winner. You can determine how many "races" to have with your student/group. Usually, after the warm-ups, a maximum of twelve to fifteen would be appropriate, depending on the amount of time you have available. (See below for an example of the game chart.)

CLIMBER	WU	WU	WU	1	2	3	4	5	6	7	8	9	10
AMY	5.9+	5.10-	5.10-	5.10	5.10	5.10+	5.10+	5.11-	5.11-	5.11	5.11	5.11	5.11+ 3:15
JEFF	5.10	5.10	5.10+	5.11+	5.12	5.12+							
NANCY	5.10+	5.10+	5.11-	5.11-	5.11-	5.11-	5.11	5.11	5.11	5.11	5.12		
BILL	5.8	5.8	5.9	5.9	5.9	5.9+	5.9+	5.10-	5.10-	5.10	5.10	5.10	5.10+ 3:05
KAREN	5.10	5.10	5.10i	5.11	5.11	5.11i	5.12	5.12	5.12	5.12	5.12	5.12i	

NOTE: WU= Warm-up

Notice that Amy was able to finish the entire race, going up steadily in the grades, not jumping around or trying to increase the difficulty too fast. Jeff, on the other hand, increased his difficulty too quickly and was unable to finish. He wasn't able to increase his grade level or complete any other 5.12+'s after his first one.

Nancy was also progressing along well, until she jumped up a grade and then couldn't complete anything of the same level to finish out the race. Bill was steady throughout the race and finished earlier than Amy, so Bill actually won this race climbing easier routes than Amy. Karen competed well until the end, then petered out and wasn't able to complete the final race, although she was one of the strongest climbers in the group and tried extremely hard.

(A big thank-you to Canadian climbers Zoe Kozub and Seth Mason for using this game during a U.S. Climbing Team Junior Camp.)

Push

While your student is climbing on an easy route—or when he is getting pumped—have the climber concentrate on using his feet to "push" his body up the climb. He should say "push" out loud whenever he steps on a hold and activates his leg muscles. He will actually use more leg muscle—which is much stronger than the arms—when he is saying the word "push." After the workout, he will know he has been using the body correctly if his legs are more sore and tired than his arms.

Resting

While bouldering on large holds, have the climber find a "rest" position on about three holds for each hand on the climb. She should drop an arm, look at the ground—opening up the shoulders—close her eyes, and tell herself to relax and breathe. Having a key word like "breathe" or "rest" will help when climbing with a partner. The partner can say the climber's key word to help trigger the reflex to rest in her body. The climber should continue climbing for a long period of time, resting as often as possible. This exercise can be timed (example: thirty minutes without touching the ground) or by completing a certain number of "laps" on the wall. This exercise will teach your student to rest and relax while climbing without coming off the wall.

Rest on Every Move

Resting is one of the most difficult things to learn. If a climber is not accustomed to resting and rushes to the top of the route, he will need to overcome that desire and learn to stop and rest. If you have climbers who typically fall a move or two from the top of routes, this is the perfect exercise for them.

A good rest position while bouldering—weight is over the feet, the resting arm is dropped toward the ground, and the climber is looking down at the ground up, with her shoulders opened up to promote blood flow. Photo: Stewart Green

Have the climber get on a route at the lower end of his onsight level. Each move that he makes must include a pause for three deep breaths before continuing on. Each time the climber moves a hand, he must adjust his body into the optimal resting position, look at the ground, take three deep breaths, and then move into the next position. Once this is mastered on easy climbs, the climber can progress to more difficult climbs, resting on holds that he feels he can barely hold onto, let alone rest on. This will teach the climber to get into good rest positions, even on difficult holds. Sometimes climbers complain that regardless of all the resting, they feel tired when they get to the top. This is probably a sign of overgripping or not fully getting into a rest position. Make sure resting is *mastered* before allowing students to get on more difficult routes.

Shake 'n' Bake

After getting completely pumped on a climb, have your student go to the bouldering wall and find one giant hold—or two holds, one for each hand. The climber should get on the hold while still pumped and stay on the hold for ten minutes without coming off the wall.

While the climber is hanging on the hold in a good rest position, she should be shaking out each hand, resting, relaxing, and stretching out the forearms. By the time she comes off the wall, she should no longer be pumped. Resting in this manner will help the student learn that she can recover, even while on a route.

Speed Climbing

Although it will seem a little funny to have your student practice this method of climbing, it is a valuable training tool. There are times when climbing slowly will hinder the climber's attempt on a climb and speed is of the essence. To do this exercise, make sure you have a competent belayer who can either bring the rope through the belay device quickly or run backward to take up the slack. There are two methods of speed climbing:

- **Paddling:** The eyes are constantly up and the climber is grabbing handholds as quickly as possible. The climber does not look down for feet, but rather "paddles" with them and hopes they land on a hold.

- **Jumping:** Both feet are moving up at once (pushing) and grabbing the handholds as they come. Again, the climber does not look at the footholds but rather lets the feet randomly land on them.

Tag

This game is a fun activity near the end of a practice, and takes several climbers. It can be a great game if you are at the gym during a busy time when there are a lot of other kids around climbing. It can last as long as you would like it to, although usually thirty minutes to an hour is sufficient. You can develop variations of this game.

Tag needs to be played in a large area, where your climbers will have access to different types of walls with a lot of holds. Climbers are not tied into the wall. The game is played while bouldering, but you must set limitations on maximum bouldering height. All climbers are allowed to get off the wall at any point to go to another wall; however they risk being tagged when they are off the wall. Start with one climber designated as "it." When the climbers are on the wall, they cannot be tagged by "it" if they are in motion. They can only be tagged when they are on the ground, switching walls, or if they are not moving on the wall. "It" must give a warning to the climber he plans to tag by counting to five. If the climber doesn't move by the count of five by actually grabbing another hold, "it" can tag the climber and that climber becomes "it." "It" is allowed to count as fast as he would like. If you have a large group, you can also have more than one "it," which will make the game more challenging. *(Thanks to my fabulous instructor, Aaron Shamy, for this great exercise.)*

Twister

Yes, it is what you are thinking—except on a climbing wall instead of a piece of plastic with small colored circles. Playing twister on the wall can be fun for everyone, no matter what level of ability each climber is at. This is a great game for a group of climbers, but it can be played with only one student.

Have all the climbers get on the wall (bouldering style/no ropes). Call out "right hand red" or any color of tape that is marking routes/boulder problems on the wall. Climbers must find a red-taped hold for their right hand. Next call out another color and another appendage, such as "left foot blue." Keep the game moving rather quickly, calling out hands or feet and colors quickly so that your students don't get bored.

You can also play this game by designating hands only and letting the climber pick her own feet.

Chapter 13: **Pyramids**

I am not talking about the pyramids of Egypt here, but go ahead and put that picture in your mind. Every coach uses a different type of pyramid. Most pyramids are meant to be long term in order to keep track of a training cycle or to keep the students from trying hard routes before they have mastered moderate routes. Two bouldering pyramids are included in Chapter 10; they can also be done on lead or TR training sessions.

Redpoint Pyramid

Redpoint pyramids are developed to increase skill for working routes (not onsight-ing). A redpoint pyramid has higher grades than a climber's onsight pyramid, but you should pick a starting level that you know the climber can onsight most of the time. The sample pyramid depicts a climber who is barely in the 5.11+ onsight range. The difficulty level on the bottom of the pyramid shows the easiest climbs, and the climbs increase in difficulty to the top of the pyramid. The top climb is the climber's goal and should be redpointed during a specified amount of time. For practical purposes, a redpoint pyramid should be developed so that the climber can see an improvement in performance in one to two months. Each cell in each row is considered complete when the climber redpoints the climb, and only then is the climber allowed to move on to the next cell. This gives the climber the practical climbing skills necessary to advance to the next level. Start at the bottom left-hand corner of the pyramid and work across before going up to the next level. Notice that the climber must redpoint three 5.11+'s before moving up to 5.12-, giving the climber "experience" before going on to a more difficult grade. The following example depicts a pyramid over a short period of time, perhaps a one- to two-month period.

REDPOINT PYRAMID EXAMPLE:

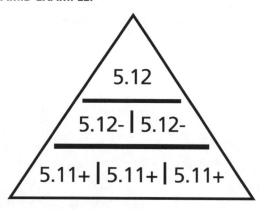

Onsight Pyramid

An onsight pyramid differs slightly from a redpoint pyramid because the climber must complete each level without falling before he can move on to the next level of onsights. In other words, he is not allowed to work harder climbs until he has mastered/onsighted each row of the pyramid. Start at the bottom left-hand corner of the pyramid and work across before going up to the next level. In the onsight pyramid example, the climber must onsight three 5.11's (base of the pyramid) before moving on to 5.11+. The climber must then onsight two 5.11+'s before attempting to onsight a 5.12-. The example below depicts an onsight pyramid for a short period of time, perhaps a one- to two-month period.

ONSIGHT PYRAMID EXAMPLE:

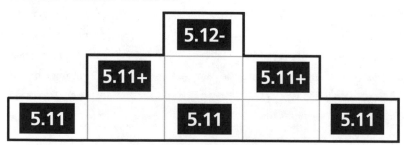

Long-term Redpoint and Onsight Pyramids

This type of pyramid will be worked on over a six-month to one-year period. The climber should have her long-term pyramid on paper to document her improvement. The goal for completing the pyramid will take time, as opposed to the previous pyramids, in which goals are reached more easily. Start at the bottom left-hand corner of the pyramid and work across before going up to the next level. As the example shows, the difficulty increases by one grade as the climber moves forward so the advancement is slower.

The climber must determine whether she is using this as an onsight or redpoint pyramid and stick with it. She should not switch back and forth between the two.

LONG-TERM REDPOINT AND ONSIGHT PYRAMIDS EXAMPLE:

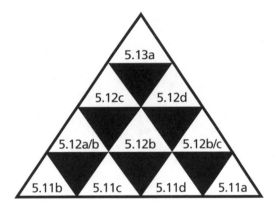

Chapter 14: **Training for Competitions**

"Your school may have done away with winners and losers, but life has not."
—Bill Gates

Types of Competitions

There are numerous types of competitions for your students to show off the skills you have taught them, which they have developed through hard work. Following is a brief description of competitions, followed by a guide on how to train specifically for each type.

In some areas, you can take your students to established competition circuits. Other organizations also offer competitions: United States Competition Climbing Association (USCCA), Professional Climbers Association (PCA), Denver Climbing League (DCL), and the American Bouldering Series (ABS). Any event you can get your climbers to attend will be helpful to improve their overall climbing. Climbing in other gyms also gives climbers a better feel for their climbing abilities, because they can make comparisons with other climbers and other routes.

All competitions are not created equal, and some are better than others. There are also different styles of competitions, even within the established competition-climbing organizations. Below are some samples of climbing competition categories, but there is by no means a standard that applies to all events across the board.

LEVELS OF COMPETITION

(General guidelines/individual gyms will vary)

Beginner: Routes up to 5.9; bouldering up to V2

Intermediate: Routes from 5.10 to 5.11; bouldering up to V4

Advanced: Routes from 5.11+ to 5.12; bouldering up to V6

Open: Routes 5.12 and up; bouldering over V6

USCCA Age Categories

(as of this writing, subject to change)

11 and under, 12–13, 14–15*, 16–17*, and 18–19*

(*ages 14–19 can attend Junior World Competition)

BOULDERING COMPETITIONS

These comps are very similar to "redpoint competitions," only without ropes. Competitors are given a list of problems and sometimes a map and are told to climb as many problems as they want. Problems must be completed to receive points. Typically the top five to ten scores will be calculated to determine the winner, but be sure to check the rules at each individual competition.

The basic strategy at a bouldering competition is to have your student warm up and then pick problems in the category she is competing in, trying to fill the scorecard as soon as possible. When the minimum number of problems has been reached, the competitor can then try to drop her lowest scores by doing harder problems. One of the biggest mistakes made in bouldering competitions is not filling the scorecard completely by not completing the minimum number of problems. Sometimes competitors will go to a bouldering competition and just try the hardest problems. Even if they get to the second to the last hold, no points are received, and energy is wasted. It is better to have lower scores than no points at all.

ONSIGHT COMPETITIONS

These competitions usually include "isolation," where the climber is not allowed to watch anyone else on the route until she has climbed it herself. Once the competitor is allowed to climb, she is usually given a set amount of time—typically at least five minutes—to complete the climb. When the climber falls, the judge determines the high point (highest handhold reached on the route), and that is the competitor's score. Some onsight competitions have multiple routes, and the climber will be

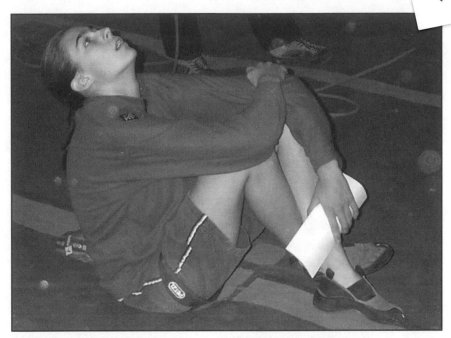

It's tough to watch the competition on a route you've already climbed. Here, Erin Axtell waits to see if her highpoint will stick. Photo: Craig Axtell

Instructor Michelle Hurni clipping at her waist during an ASCF national competition. Photo: Rod Willard

led from route to route. Climbs must be done in the order designated by the judge and may have a rest period between problems.

REDPOINT COMPETITIONS

These are probably the least intimidating competitions around, but can be a bit confusing and may even seem disorganized at first glance. In this type of competition the climber can take a number of attempts to complete a route, with credit given only if the route is finished. Climbers are often responsible for filling out their own scorecard and are on the honor system. Sometimes competitors will be offered a number of routes to chose from, and the top five scores are counted. This is the best introduction to competition climbing, because the competitor gets to pick the climbs. For seasoned competitors, however, there is a strategy involved. The climber completes five routes on the scorecard and then eliminates the lowest scores by climbing only harder problems for the remainder of the competition.

SPEED CLIMBING COMPETITIONS

These events are usually held in conjunction with onsight or redpoint competitions. In a speed climbing event, the climber is tied into a toprope. When the signal is given to begin climbing, the competitors go as fast as possible to the top of the wall—drag race style. The routes are typically easy (5.6–5.8). The climber who

Two climbers racing to the top of the speed climbing wall in Imst, Austria.
Photo: Craig Axtell

reaches the top of the wall first wins. These events are usually set up in a "brack-eted" format so that the climber with the fastest time will advance from round to round. At smaller competitions top times determine the winner and are based on only one or two individual runs. The ESPN X Games have a speed climbing competition each summer that offers the highest prize purse of any climbing event in the United States.

SPEED DIFFICULTY COMPETITIONS

These are timed competitions offered in conjunction with difficulty events. The climber must attempt a difficult route—usually at least 5.11+ on lead—against the clock. The climber with the quickest time to the top of the wall with no falls wins.

Training for Competitions

Training for climbing competitions takes an intense dedication. In order for an athlete to do well on the competition circuit, the climber must be willing to devote at least fifteen hours of training time per week to the sport. This means training time is spent climbing, not horsing around, and it must be taken seriously. The climber should also be having enough fun during training sessions to remain dedicated.

There are many aspects to training for competitions, including journaling, goal setting, training methods, the competition mindset, and preparation for competition climbing. Each aspect is discussed in length in this chapter.

Journaling

One of the best ways to see improvement in a training cycle is to journal during every climbing session, whether training or just climbing for fun. Your student may think she is not improving, but if she can see it in on paper, she will be encouraged by even the smallest gains. Sit down and talk with your student, make sure she understands what she needs to keep track of.

A journal is a great way to keep track of workouts and determine what your student needs to work on in the future. It will also be a reference of what she has accomplished over a period of time. She may not see an increase in grades, but she may see an increase in workout intensity, which will lead to an increase in grades.

Have your students keep a journal listing the following items for each workout:

- The amount of time spent climbing.

- The number of routes and moves completed. Specify whether they were lead climbs, toproped climbs, or boulder problems, and list the difficulty of each climb.

- The reason a move was difficult or impossible to complete—for example, too reachy or too pumped to make the move.

- How they feel at the end of the workout—for example, tired, pumped, good.

- Any other thoughts they would like to write down that might help them remember the workout.

SAMPLE JOURNAL ENTRY:

Date: September 10, Tuesday—first day after two rest days
3:30–6:00 P.M. Power-endurance workout

During warm-up I led two 5.10+'s back to back, and then my partner climbed. Next I led a 5.11- and a 5.10+ back to back and didn't fall. The 5.10+ was a little difficult after the 5.11-.

After warming up I did a mini-pyramid.
1. Red 5.11 on steep wall. No falls and it didn't feel difficult.
2. Blue 5.11+ on 30° wall. A bit balancy near the top and I almost fell.
3. Green 5.12- on 30° wall. Got to the last draw and was too pumped to clip.
4. Green 5.12- (again). Rested and completed the route.
5. Yellow 5.12. Got 3/4 of the way up and fell because I was too pumped, even though I had just clipped a draw.
6. Yellow 5.12 (again). Got two moves higher, but still didn't make it to the top, even after shaking out and resting on the rope.
7. Green 5.12-. Hung once—too pumped going back down the pyramid.
8. Blue 5.11+ on 30° wall. Fell in the balancy section.
9. Red 5.11 on steep. No falls but pumped and tired.

Cool down on 5.10+ from warm-up—three consecutive laps falling a few feet lower on each one, all on TR.

At the end of the workout I could barely untie my shoes I was so pumped! Climbed a total of 16 climbs and fell 5 times.

Look at the journal entry here and see if you can pinpoint what this climber needs to be working on. I see two obvious things: (1) power-endurance—more than one route at a time—because she is falling close to the top of each climb and (2) technical climbing for balance.

Goals

"The only one standing in the way of your goals is you."

Each of your students needs to answer a set of questions to determine where he is in his training cycle and to decide what is important to accomplish. Have each student sit down and answer the following questions, and then work together on setting goals—short and long term—with each individual climber.

1. Do I have any climbing trips planned for the next three months? If so, where is the trip to, and what do I want to accomplish during the trip?

2. Are there any competitions coming up? If so, what type of competitions are they, and how important are they to me?

3. What level am I redpointing right now?

4. What level am I onsighting right now?

5. What level do I want to be redpointing in three months? One year?

6. What level do I want to be onsighting in three months? One year?

7. What is my main strength, favorite type of climbing?

8. What is my major weakness, least favorite type of climbing?

9. How many days a week can I commit to a training program? How many hours per day can I commit to meeting my goals?

10. When do I want to take a two-week break from climbing so my body can recover?

As soon as those questions are answered and discussed, keep the following in mind before setting goals for each climber:

1. Make the goals reasonable and attainable.

2. Don't set goals so low that the climber can attain them halfway through the training period. You want the student to be able to reach the goals, but it should be something the climber has to work for.

3. Make sure the entire training regiment is set forth on paper—climbing, aerobic, stretching, etc.—so that each element is part of the end result.

4. Have the student take part in the goal-setting so that it is something she wants for herself and not something you are dictating that she has to attain.

5. Keep track of the big picture. If the climber gets injured, adjust the goals so that he is not disappointed when the goals are not reached because of the injury.

SETTING INDIVIDUAL GOALS FOR CLIMBING

The first step in goal-setting is to determine the end result desired. Is it to achieve a specific grade level? Should goals be related to performance at grade level or endurance? If the most important goal to the student is to be prepared for a climbing trip in two months at Red Rocks (outside Las Vegas), then the goal must reflect that. For example: "My goal is to climb short sport routes at Red Rocks." (Most climbs are ten draws or shorter—in the 45-foot range.) In this case, the climber should be working on crimpers, slightly overhanging lead routes. Set the goal to work out four times per week, redpointing routes that are around 45 feet long. The climber must have a foundation to support the goal. If the student is going to Red Rocks on a sport climbing trip and all she does is boulder, she will be unlikely to meet her goals.

Have the climber help set goals that are attainable for her. Then make any adjustments you feel are necessary to keep her motivated and push her to her full climbing potential.

GOAL-SETTING TIPS FOR ROPED COMPETITION

- Goals will be onsight oriented, even if some of the competitions are redpoint format. It's always better to get a route on the first try than to have to go back and waste energy climbing it again.

- The climber needs to attain a grade level (or two) higher than the expected level of competition routes. If you know the routes at a regional level competition are going to be 5.12b, make sure your climber is able to onsight at that level or higher.

- Goals should be accomplished in time for the most important competition of the season. The goal should not be set so that the climber has reached his peak in April for an event in June—it can cause burnout if the climber tries to maintain that top level of performance for three months. It's okay to build up past the goal if the climber is strong enough, but if that peak is a high level for that individual climber, it is possible that he will not be able to maintain at that level for a long period of time. Build up all aspects of climbing so that the climber is ready for the *most* important event. Don't worry about somewhat insignificant local events if the climber's goal is to do well at a national.

- Set intermediate goals for each competition along the way. Determine which category the climber will be competing in, and make sure she can reach the ratings set within that category.

- Set the training schedule to meet the goals. If the climber needs to improve two number levels in two months, the training schedule is going to have to be extremely intense for the goal to be reached.

- If it is obvious midway through the training cycle that the goals set at the beginning of the cycle will not be reached, reevaluate the goals and determine if they need to be changed.

GOAL-SETTING TIPS FOR OUTDOOR BOULDERING

- If the goal is to boulder outside as hard as possible, the climber needs to work power-endurance and power and to climb outside as often as possible to become familiar with climbing on natural rock.

- Goals for climbing outside range from the number of problems completed to the grade/difficulty of problems. Determine which is the main goal. Some boulderers might say, "I want to climb every V5 at my local area," and other boulderers might say, "I want to climb a V10."

- If the goal is a grade, the climber should make sure he is up to climbing that grade. If the goal is V10 and the climber has only worked one V8, then the goal needs to be progressive: ten V8's, twelve V9's, and then move up to V10. The dues must be paid, and the more a climber practices problems at what he feels is "below his ability," the easier his body will adapt to harder problems.

- If the goal is grade and the climber is able to onsight boulder problems at one grade below his goal, he has a reasonable goal. The first goal is to pick a problem that suits the climber. If a climber is good with slopers, then a sloper problem of the "goal" grade may be the best problem to work. If a climber is good at crimpers and picks a sloper problem, it will take longer to accomplish the goal.

- Pure saturation of routes is a great goal, and the climber needs to pick a grade that is reasonable for his climbing ability—for example V7. At this point, the climber should warm up and then try to do as many V7's during a session as possible. Keeping track of the number of tries on any given day can chart his improvement within the grade. With a journal, he can keep track of the type of problems he is climbing and try to get in a variety—slopey, crimpy, overhanging, etc.—of problems so that his overall climbing will benefit.

- One important aspect of setting goals for bouldering is to remember that the grades are subjective. Not all V7's are alike—some are endurance, some are power, and some are sandbagged.

GOAL-SETTING TIPS FOR BOULDERING COMPETITIONS

- Bouldering competitions are typically pretty relaxed, and the climber is able to climb the problems in whatever order she wants. There are two ways to go about setting goals for bouldering competitions:

  1) The first goal that can be set is the number of problems. A climber can set the goal of climbing every route in her category. If this is the climber's goal, she should make sure to warm up properly, then commence bouldering. She should start at the lower end of the climbs in her category, get a feel for the problems, and then get on some of the harder problems. The biggest mistake made in bouldering competitions is getting on hard problems too quickly, burning out, and being unable to climb more problems.

  2) The other option for bouldering competitions is climbing all the hardest problems possible. In this option, the climber needs to make sure he is properly warmed up so that he doesn't get a "flash pump."

- Goals can be set before the bouldering competitions—for example, a goal of bouldering at least V6 consistently. In this case, the climber needs to train on many problems one grade below the V6 goal. Then he should work up to V6 and get in as many as possible until the grade feels reasonable.

- Bouldering competitions are typically set up so that the climber must climb a set number of problems. Make sure your climber gets in the minimum number of climbs before moving on to work the really hard problems just for points. Points are needed to be competitive and place well, but if he is working too hard and unable to complete the problems, there will be no points.

Training Cycles for Competition

Training cycles can vary depending on the objectives. Two basic training cycles can be used: "training to peak" and "overall conditioning."

TRAINING TO PEAK

When a climber trains to "peak," each training aspect—endurance, power-endurance, and power—is worked to perfection, and then the climber moves on to the next phase. This type of training brings the climber to a "peak performance" at a specific time. For example, the climber may spend one month climbing only endurance routes and then move on to power-endurance for the next month. For the final month in the cycle, the climber advances to power training.

The downside to this type of training is that the peak typically doesn't last very long—maybe a week. If the climber is training for a competition that is three months away, that peak has to happen at a specific point. If the climber misses that point and peaks one weekend before the competition or one weekend after, the whole cycle is wasted for that competition. The other downside to training to peak is that the months during the cycle are all spent training specific aspects of climbing; the climber will not climb well on a powerful climb if she is on her endurance cycle.

Another downfall is boredom. A climber on the peak training cycle who is working only endurance for a specified period of time can get bored and lose motivation. Various forms of climbing are not combined during the cycles, and climbing the same type of route each day can become monotonous. If you chose to train your student in this style, be creative with your practice structure.

Theoretically, as the cycle progresses, each aspect of climbing becomes stronger until the end of the cycle, when the climber has achieved peak physical form and fitness. For example, at the end of the endurance cycle, the climber is a fantastic endurance climber. At the completion of the twelve-week cycle, power and endurance meet to form one completely fit climber. After the climber has peaked, a long rest must be taken before the cycle can begin again. Obviously the climber will not be starting from the same place at the beginning of the next cycle, because the previous cycle will have improved his overall fitness level.

Following is an example of a training-to-peak cycle, with the performance level indicated as increasing from week to week. Note how quickly all of the elements begin to decline after the climber has peaked and the body is exhausted from the cycle.

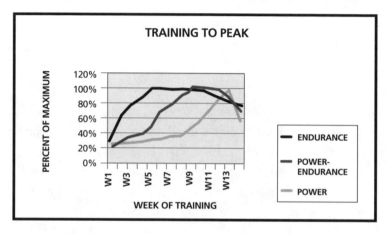

OVERALL CONDITIONING

If a climber decides on a training cycle to include all aspects of climbing, the performance level of all aspects will increase gradually, as opposed to one aspect at a time in the training-to-peak cycle. A training cycle for overall improvement takes into account a weekly or monthly training cycle, with the student climbing one to two days "on," and then one to two days "off" (resting).

In this type of cycle, the first day "on" will be the more difficult of the two days, although it can be the shorter day. For example, day one will be power and day two will be power-endurance. The climber then takes two days off, and then the next day may be power-endurance, with the second day being endurance. Never will there be two days of endurance, or two days of power in a row, keeping the cycle more varied than "training to peak." If a student climbs just one day on, it should be a pretty hard day of training power or hard power-endurance. Sometimes a climber's schedule may be such that the climber always climbs one day on and one day off. If this is the case, he can rotate through the cycle—day one power, day two off, day three power-endurance, day four off, day five endurance, day six and seven off, or something to that effect.

The curve of improvement during an overall training cycle will look slower than the peak training curve, but the overall objective is the same—to become a better conditioned climber. The main difference between these two types of training cycles is that the overall training cycle is not as tedious and that the climber is able to get on challenging routes throughout the cycle as each element comes into play.

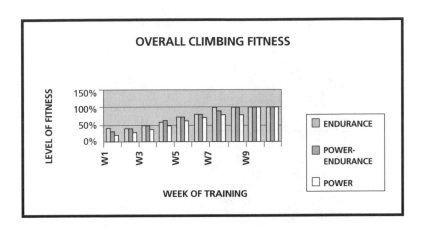

The Competition Brain

"If you mess up, it's not your parents' fault, so don't whine about your mistakes, learn from them."
—Bill Gates

Perhaps one of the most difficult issues to deal with in competition climbing is the brain working against the climber before and during an event. The following competition tips can ease a climber's mindset:

- Make sure the climber understands what he can and cannot control. He should decide what is within his control: eating and drinking properly before climbing, warming up, dressing properly, playing music on a Walkman to relax, etc. He also needs to determine what is out of his control: the temperature within the building, running order, amount of rest between climbs, etc. Have him make a list of worries and then put those things that cannot be controlled out of his mind. By taking the things he can control and making them as perfect as possible, much of the anxiety level will be decreased. Hold a "mock" competition ahead of time and make sure everyone is warming up properly, resting enough between problems, has enough food and water, etc.

Receiving instructions from the judge, Erin Axtell is tied in and ready to onsight at a JCCA competition. Notice the start holds in the blue taped box on the wall behind them. Photo: Craig Axtell

- Your climber must show up on time for the competition and know the running order and format. If you can get the schedule ahead of time and do some practice competitions, the format/setting will be more familiar when it's time for competition.

- Find out who the other competitors are and know what your student is up against. If the competition is stiff, he needs to understand that he will have to be on top of his game, trying his hardest. If the competition is easy, he should understand that he still must concentrate and that focus is still needed to win, but he may not have to go all out to win. Competitions, however, are unpredictable; there can sometimes be an unknown factor that you have not prepared for—such as a new climber to the scene who is cranking!

- Set a goal before the competition, but be flexible with that goal. If it is a three-round competition—qualifier, semifinal, and final—your student should focus on getting to the next round. For example, in the qualifier the goal should be to make it to the semifinal. Make sure your climber doesn't set a goal of winning the competition before it even begins so that he isn't crushed if he makes a mistake and does not make it past the qualifier. A better goal would be to concentrate on getting to the next round or winning each round. Small steps will get him farther than attempts at giant leaps.

- Find out what helps the student relax, and practice it during training sessions. If you have a student who gets tense while climbing in a competition, focus on relaxation techniques during training sessions. Set your student up to climb in tense situations and then practice relaxing. However, it is nearly impossible to duplicate the tension at a climbing competition.

- Have your student talk to other competitors to find out what helps them to relax and try their tactics.

- Make sure your student doesn't wear himself out during warm-up. It can be fun to climb with his buddies in isolation, but make sure he doesn't get carried away—he can climb more after the competition.

- Your student should warm up properly during the allotted time so that he does not get "flash pumped" when competing. Make sure he has warmed up for at least twenty minutes to get the muscles slightly pumped, and then stretch, rest, and climb again. If he is in isolation and gets a good pump, make sure he has cleared out the lactic acid buildup by stretching out the upper body/forearms before going out to climb.

- Have your student drink lots of water and go to the bathroom before putting on his harness. There is always a last-minute dash to the toilet, but make sure it doesn't turn into a rush to get to the route on time.

- Your climber should do one of two things with the crowd noise: Either listen to the crowd for positive reinforcement, or block out the noise. A climber who needs to block out the noise should practice focusing only on the climb and not the crowd. Make sure, however, that if you have a climber who doesn't like to hear the crowd when she climbs that it doesn't turn into a distraction or disadvantage.

- Remind your student to focus completely on the task at hand but remember to have a good time. Help him relax so that he doesn't get so uptight about a competition that he gets physically ill. Remind him that if he makes a mistake, chances are he is the only one who will remember it. One competition does not make or break a climbing career. There will always be other competitions.

- Encourage your student to take a look around the crowd as she walks out to the climb, maybe wave to friends or say hello to her parents. Those people are there to support that climber, no matter how well she does. The spectators are probably just as nervous as the climber, but their feelings don't count when the climber is up on the wall. If the climber is prepared for the competition, the crowd should not matter.

- Try to get your climber into an ideal performance state—determine what is paramount for him so that he can perform at his best. The way he performs is a direct reflection of how he feels inside. Have him create a checklist of his emotions to determine if he needs to change something before climbing: alert state, optimism, control, mental calm, anxiety level, mental focus, happy, relaxed, energized, self-confident.

- Discuss a time when she performed at her best. Duplicate that moment whenever possible for repeat results. Ask these questions to help determine that ideal state: What did you do to achieve that performance level? What was happening in your life? What did you eat beforehand? Did you get enough sleep?

Preparing for a Competition

PRIOR TO THE COMPETITION

- A few weeks before the competition, find out what type of warm-up area will be available to your student. If there is only a small bouldering area available, make sure you have your climber warm up only bouldering for the week or two preceding the competition for familiarity. The body needs time to adjust if the climber will be warming up in an unfamiliar way.

- The entire week before the competition should be spent climbing very easy, low-level climbs during practice. "Cramming" is not appropriate in the week before a competition—if the climber is not ready at that point, resting the muscles will be the best remedy.

- There should be no climbing for two days prior to the competition. This needs to be strictly enforced so that your climber will be well rested. Specifically, if there is a competition on Saturday, the last climbing day is Wednesday. Thursday and Friday are *rest* days.

- Prepare for the competition—know the format, sign-in time, what time isolation closes, etc.

- Know how long it takes to get to the competition so that your student is not late. There is no excuse for being late for a competition.

- If you have to travel to the competition, plan on arriving with enough time to get a good night's sleep the night before.

- Try not to put any additional stress on the climber by being unprepared.

- The night before the competition, make sure the climber eats a good meal and relaxes.

AT THE COMPETITION

What happens the day of a competition can be the difference between first and last place. Make sure your climber arrives psyched to climb. A little nervousness is okay, but make sure it doesn't overshadow the training that has gone into making this one of the best climbing days of the season.

- Showing up on time and knowing the format of the event is the easiest part of the day. Check the running order if it is an onsight competition. If it is a bouldering event, make sure you and your student know exactly how many routes she will be scored on completing.

- Be prepared—your climber should have everything she needs, including reading materials, climbing gear, food, water, CD or tape player, extra batteries, and plenty of clothing.

- Eat before competing if possible, but make sure it isn't junk! There is no reason for a climber to "carbo load." Just make sure your climber has some fruit, a bagel, or something relatively healthy a few hours before the competition. She needs to have fuel in the body so it doesn't crash right before competing, but it shouldn't be so heavy that it weighs her down.

Finding this ideal (but unusual) rest, Tommy Caldwell takes full advantage of it.
Photo: Stewart Green

- Once the competition starts, make sure your student knows what is expected of her. Is she climbing three routes in a row with no rest? Does she climb the first route, get a five minute rest, and then climb another route?

- Mental preparation is key when on the route(s). Coach your student to climb as hard as she can. If she needs to pretend it's just another session in the gym, that's okay. Relaxing while climbing is one of the most important strategies on the wall—let the body and training take over.

I once came out for the semifinal at a national event and blew it. I ended up finishing close to last. After my climb, I sat down next to my fellow competitor, Lizz Grenard, and she said she knew as soon as she saw how white my face was that I was going to fall early. I had been so focused on doing well that I literally psyched myself out of the competition. My body was tense (I got pumped); the moves looked hard (I overgripped). Here I was at a national event in the best shape of my career; I should have finished in the top five, and I could barely climb! *Focus is good, but relaxation is better.*

Sample Workout from a Professional Climber

Below are two weeks of sample workouts for competition training. You can vary these depending on what type of competition is coming up.

DAY ONE, WEEK ONE

The first training day should be spent on the most difficult aspect of training, the most taxing type of training on the body—power. At the gym during this workout, your student needs to boulder to get a true "power" workout. You will need to have numerous problems available for his ability level. After warming up for about twenty minutes—either bouldering or toproping—either make up boulder problems or use problems someone else has made up for you. For one hour, after your student has warmed up sufficiently, have him work on an hour glass pyramid (Chapter 10, Bouldering Games and Activities).

The rest between each attempt should be one to three minutes—depending on the difficulty. This will give the climber five actual problems—two relatively easy and three hard; he will actually do eighteen laps total. This pyramid should take at least two hours to complete.

If the climber gets to problem five too quickly, add in one more extremely difficult problem that the climber has to work out the moves on but probably cannot send. Theoretically, by the time the climber starts back down the pyramid, the body should know the problems. However, the muscles will be tired, and the climber may not be able to complete the easier problems as quickly on the way back down.

DAY TWO, WEEK ONE

This workout should be a little less difficult than Day One, so power-endurance is the best training method for this session. Your student should warm up completely before the one-and-a-half- to two-hour toprope or lead training session begins. If your student is leading, make sure he is leading at his limit after the moderate climbs!

- To warm up, have him onsight as many new routes—at least three—as are available in the gym on this day. If three new routes are not available, have him climb slightly harder routes he has already completed but can now redpoint without falling.

- After that, he should get on a bit harder routes at his onsight/redpoint break. He should climb as many routes as possible, with a maximum of three to five minutes between routes. This should last at least forty-five minutes—more if he feels good and has the time. Try to have your climber get in at least six hard routes.

- The difficulty of the routes should gradually increase, and on the "hard routes" the climber should barely make it to the top or fall very close to the top. The climber should have to work and push to complete these routes.

- When there are fifteen minutes left, your climber needs to pick a route that was somewhat difficult for him. At this point in the workout, he should barely be able to do the route. There should not be an obvious crux, and the route should be pretty sustained. He will do the route one time, get lowered to the ground either upon reaching the top or when he falls, and rest one minute. He will then do the route a second time, get lowered to the ground (he should not have gotten to the top on this lap, and should be lowered as soon as he falls), and rest another minute. He will now do the route a third and final time, and get lowered to the ground when he falls. If he is able to complete the route each time, it is too easy; you need to pick a harder route for him.

- Depending on the time left, pick another route that is slightly easier, and have the climber do three more laps. This exercise will build power-endurance, and the climber should not be resting on any holds—he should be pushing to the top or just through one more move. By taking a one-minute rest and then doing the same route again engrams are built up, and he should be able to push through moves the second and third times on the route. The goal of this exercise is to mentally push through the moves, even when tired, and try to do the route without falling. Remember, though, if the climber does the route without falling on any of the three laps, it is too easy and is not pushing the climber enough for power-endurance. You are not trying to build endurance, but rather power-endurance—endurance on harder routes, where the climber actually has to push to complete them.

DAY THREE, WEEK ONE

The third day, after at least one rest day, will be bouldering. This workout should be an easier version of power-endurance. Mainly, have your student work on resting—finding a good rest position and recovering before continuing to climb.

Set a circular boulder problem that is difficult to complete, but the climber should be able to make it back to the start/finish hold without falling. You can make these problems by starting with a good hold, making ten to fourteen moves that are difficult for the climber that lead back to the good hold she can rest on before doing another lap.

- Have your student start by warming up with boulder problems fifteen to twenty moves long, completing each problem twice to build engrams. Again, have her start easy and graduate to harder and harder problems. The problems should be twenty to thirty moves long. This section of the workout should last at least forty-five minutes, and the climber should be sufficiently warmed up and getting pumped.

- Another great exercise for this day is tied-together leading, which requires two students. Set up approximately eight quick draws around the bouldering cave, tie two climbers together with a 10-foot piece of rope, and have them boulder around the cave with one draw always clipped between them. Make sure each person takes a turn "leading" and "following."

- If you have a "solo" session with only one student, she can do the above problem with a short rope tied around her waist and climb around the boulder, clipping each quick draw as she traverses the boulder. This is "simulated leading" and will get her accustomed to getting into proper clipping positions as she climbs.

- Make sure your student is watching the quick draw each time she clips, using proper clipping stances and resting whenever possible.

- Near the end of the workout have the climber get on the circular "rest" problem. Set a goal of completing the circle a certain number of times; three to six laps is a good goal, depending on the difficulty of the problem. The moves should be difficult, but the climber should not fall the first couple of times around. The main goal of this boulder problem is to feel recovery on the rest hold before continuing on the next lap.

DAY ONE, WEEK TWO

This workout is another power workout; it is the first workout of the week, preceded by two rest days.

- This time, have your student warm up on ten more boulder problems. The warm-up should last approximately twenty minutes.

- For the warm-up, if you have more than one student in a session, pair the students into groups of two or three. The first climber makes up an easy warm-up problem, climbs it, and then has the second climber in the group climb it. The second climber now makes up and climbs a different problem, and then climber one climbs it. The climbers rotate through until they have climbed approximately six problems with each rotation getting more difficult.

- During the warm-up, find four problems that are difficult for your student. When the warm-up is complete, have your student do two sets of 4x4's (see Chapter 11, Power-Endurance Games and Activities).

The final twenty to thirty minutes should be spent on negatives or systems training. This is a fantastic way to improve technique, muscular endurance, and muscular memory.

Negatives/Systems Training:

- Pick a really good hold for your student to start on, but make sure you can find an equally good hold for the other hand. Start by having the student lock off on the hold with his feet on the wall. Hold the position for a count to five, and then slowly lower back down to a straight-arm position. Your climber should *stay on the hold* and then repeat the move—hold the position for a count of five, *slowly* lower back down, and repeat the move. He should do as many as five repetitions and as few as three per arm. Move to the other jug and do the same move on the other arm.

- On the second round, have the climber pull up to another hold, reach for the hold, but count to three before grabbing the hold. Reverse the move slowly, then repeat—again as few as three and as many as five repetitions per arm.

- Get the climber on the big hold again and have him pull across his body to lock off (to the left), lower down to the start position and pull as high as possible straight up, lower down to the start position, push backward to the right, and then lower slowly back to the start position. Have him do three sets on each arm. The hand and footholds should stay the same, but the climber should be extending as far as possible. Repeat with the opposite arm.

DAY TWO, WEEK TWO

This session includes another power-endurance bouldering workout in the bouldering area.

- Your climber should warm up on toprope doing a few easy routes—no more than three.

- For power-endurance, pair up your students to play an advanced game of add on (see Chapter 11, Power-Endurance Games and Activities, "Add On, Version Two").

- If you only have one student, you can be climber two and just go through the moves without actually climbing. This will give your student a more intense workout, as the wait between "laps" will be less without you actually climbing the problems.

- After playing a few rounds of this, have your climber go back to the beginning and do as much of the problem as he can remember from start to finish. He can tape the problem for a long power-endurance route.

DAY THREE, WEEK TWO

This session should be an endurance/power-endurance workout and will be done in the bouldering area.

- The climber should start by warming up, make up a boulder problem fifteen to twenty moves, climb it once, and then repeat it from memory. The warm-up should take approximately twenty minutes and include at least three to five problems.

- Have the climber do her resting problem from the Day Three, Week One workout. This should take approximately ten to fifteen minutes, with the climber doing at least three to five laps without stepping off the wall. This exercise is essential for developing good resting positions and feeling muscular recovery.

- Some longer problems, twenty to twenty-four moves, should be set up on the bouldering wall. These problems should not be too difficult, and your student should get through them on the first try. After she has done these problems once, she should then "lead" the routes. Attach a short piece of rope to her waist, with quick draws set up to clip along the problem.

On a twenty-four-move problem, she should have at least four quick draws to clip. This will build up endurance and help with clipping confidence. Between each problem, she should be resting for at least three minutes to fully recover before starting the next problem. Set the goal of completing at least five to seven "lead climbs" for your student.

Chapter 15:
The Excuses and Counterexcuses

"A climber who wants to do something will find a way; a climber who doesn't finds an excuse."

My general response about excuses is that there shouldn't be any. Any student using excuses to get out of training, to not train hard, or to make amends for falling off of a route needs to learn how to climb better. Excuses are a way to get out of doing something, and if a climber wants to become better, excuses will hinder that advancement. Most excuses can be handled with a new training tactic—work the weaknesses and the excuses should diminish. The example excuses in this chapter may not always be voiced in this way, but even if they are unspoken or phrased differently there are some practical ways to deal with them and these guidelines will help.

This section will come in handy during training sessions, so remember to refer to it if you are unable to respond when an excuse comes up. You will find explanations for many of the exercises mentioned in this section explained in detail throughout this book.

The following excuses have been divided into sections and grouped together based on the premise of the complaint: Attitude, Body Awareness, Mental Discomfort, Technical Difficulty, and Technique.

Attitude

"I CAN'T DO IT."

1. Have the climber take a break from the route/problem. Overtraining on a particular route or series of moves can lead to the feeling of not being able to complete a route. Sometimes a week or so off a route can make a huge difference in success or failure. If the route is just too difficult, you may want to adjust the difficulty of the climbs the student is trying to work or onsight. Some climbers set their sights too high and may become frustrated by too much failure.

2. On the other hand, the climber may just be giving up, which creates an entirely different series of counterexcuses. As the coach, you should be able to tell if a climber is giving it her best effort or just giving up—attempting the move without putting any effort into actually sticking it. If the student is just giving up, you will need to work on her motivation. Some climbers will use the "I hate that type of move" excuse (see examples) when what they are really saying is "I don't feel like doing it." Make sure you look at the entire issue and analyze it from that perspective. If it is an issue of being afraid to fall or looking bad in front of their friends, then deal with those issues.

Body Awareness

"MY SKIN HURTS."

Students can climb through skin pain unless there are visible tears and blood—in which case the open wounds should be dealt with and allowed to heal. A little red, raw skin should not be a reason to stop a workout. Climbing on new holds, or doing big moves, can make the skin on the hands/fingers hurt. There is really no way to avoid this, except to teach your students how to care for their skin by keeping it as moist as possible after climbing to avoid cracks and tears. Vitamin E oil works well to help keep the skin in good condition and is available in many forms. Dry skin will crack more easily and will be more sensitive than well-moisturized tissue.

"I'M TOO TIRED."

1. If this is just an excuse not to climb, perhaps you need to evaluate the climber's attitude.

2. If the climber is indeed too physically tired to climb, he risks injury climbing while fatigued and should take a break. This excuse can be an indicator that the climber needs his semiannual, two-week break from climbing, especially if he is continuously fatigued and not improving. Even if the climber has an

important event/competition on the horizon, a break from climbing will do him more good than pushing himself to the point of a backslide—a decrease in improvement or pushing to injury. Be aware of this trend and try to schedule a shorter training period during the next cycle, such as a two-month cycle with a two-week break instead of a three-month cycle before a break.

"MY TENDON (SHOULDER, FINGER, ELBOW) HURTS."

Test the area immediately for tenderness and swelling in the tendon. Have the climber stop climbing for the day and ice the area (see "Injury Prevention and Treatment" in Chapter 16 for more information). The student should avoid climbing for a minimum of two weeks if there is any pain at all.

"I'VE CLIMBED FOUR DAYS ON, I'M TIRED."

The climber needs to take at least two rest days. The muscles and tendons need that amount of time to recover, but if the climber has been climbing four days in a row, he may need even more time off. Performance will go downhill until the climber has fully recovered from overtraining. A climber should train a maximum of three days in a row because overtraining can cause damage to the body and mind. Some climbers are of the opinion that the more they climb, the quicker they will improve, when in fact overtraining can cause a plateau or backslide in climbing ability.

Mental Discomfort

"I'M TOO SCARED TO FALL."

1. Assuming this is a lead-climbing situation, assess whether the fall is dangerous. Make sure the climber is able to trust his belayer as some belayers do not instill confidence in the climber. Uncertainty is the last thing a climber needs to be thinking about, especially if he is making a difficult move or clip.

2. If the climber does not normally have a problem with falling, work through the issue with him to determine exactly why he is afraid to fall on this particular move. Is it a problem with the angle—too steep or too slabby? Has he had a bad fall recently that he needs to work beyond?

3. If this issue comes up frequently, the climber may need to do some "simulated leading," climbing on toprope while trailing a lead rope and practice

falling close to the ground with the lead rope just trailing. He can then practice taking lead falls: going one hold above the bolt and falling, then going two holds above the bolt and falling, then three holds, etc. With each hold farther from the quick draw, the belayer should give out a little more slack. The climber can also get to the next bolt, pull up some rope, and then let go to simulate falling with slack out for a clip. This should give the climber more confidence in falling, eliminating the "scared" issue when he sees he won't get hurt taking lead falls.

4. Some climbers will never fully get over this issue and may always be scared. If this is the case, they need to work beyond their fears and make sure they can push themselves hard enough, even with that fear. The book *Thinking Body, Dancing Mind* is a great reference for getting into the proper mental state for challenging activities.

"I CAN'T MAKE THE CLIP."

Clipping needs to be accomplished from any position, on any hold. This excuse warrants a few weeks' worth of clipping practice: climbing routes at her onsight level, clipping each draw off the right hand, and then climbing the route again, clipping off the left hand. Check out the clipping exercises in Chapter 12 and make sure the entire focus is on making the clip, not on making the moves after the clip. The climber needs to focus on one task at a time—in this case, clipping. If a climber wants to improve, clipping cannot be an excuse. Some clips are difficult, but they should not be the end of the route for the climber.

While it is acceptable to skip clips during onsight and redpoint attempts, it should not be encouraged on a regular basis; even then, it should only be encouraged in absolute 100 percent safe situations and never in a competition.

"I'M TOO SCARED TO DO THE MOVE."

This can be addressed by having the climber toprope the climb first, master the move, and then lead it. Usually it is a mental block; if the climber can successfully complete the move numerous times on toprope, he will gain the confidence to lead it. Make sure falling on this move is not dangerous before allowing the student to lead it.

"I CAN DO THE MOVE ON TOPROPE BUT NOT ON LEAD."

If the climber has worked the move on toprope and tries unsuccessfully to do the move on lead, make sure it is a safe fall. Let the climber rest on the rope two holds before doing the move and then try the move again. If the student is still too scared to do the move on lead, have her clip the draw above and work the move over and over again on toprope until it is mastered. Once it is mastered, she needs to take a long break, at least twenty minutes, and try it again. Sometimes breaking down the climb into zones for rest can make a huge difference.

"I CAN'T COMMIT TO THE MOVE."

The ability to commit to hard moves—especially off the deck when bouldering or high on the wall during a lead climb—can be a major issue. Have the climber simulate the move on a bouldering wall, close to the ground, to build up confidence. This is a mental issue, and the climber needs to do the move on toprope until it is so engrained that it is not even difficult. If this is a problem while bouldering, the climber may need to work on his mental focus in a different setting with meditation or through yoga or Tai-Chi. The book *Thinking Body, Dancing Mind* is a fantastic guide to mental training, even though it is not a climbing-related book.

Technical Difficulty

"I WAS SHORT ROPED."

For this excuse, look carefully at the belayer and make sure he knows how to lead belay. Many belayers hold the climber too tight (short rope), which can be a problem if the climber needs that extra rope for a dynamic move or a clip. Also look at the climber and make sure this isn't just an excuse. The climber needs to be responsible for communicating with the belayer and letting the belayer know what she expects. If the climber likes to feel the pressure of the rope as she climbs, she needs to vocalize that information to the belayer and also communicate when slack is needed. On the other hand, if the climber hates knowing the rope is there, the belayer needs to make sure the climber has enough slack for every move.

"IT'S TOO HOT/COLD."

Heat can be a problem in a climbing gym without a good air-conditioning system.

Being too cold should never hinder the climber, as the cooler the temperature, the better the skin sticks to holds—slopey holds can be held better on a cold day than a hot one. If it is too hot, the student will be sweating more and can slide off holds. You may need to change the time of day in which the climber is training so that the temperature is cooler. Other alternatives include wearing fewer/lighter weight clothes and bringing a personal fan.

"THE ROUTE/GYM IS BAD."

This can be a legitimate problem; however, if a climber wants to improve, it is not a viable excuse. Bad routes will make the student a better climber, as he will have to work harder to climb them. If the gym you are coaching at has bad routes, or it is just a bad gym without a lot of variety in terrain, travel to other gyms to give your student more experience. Again, make sure the route is actually bad. If it is a fluke and most of the routes are good, change climbs.

Technique

"MY HAND/FOOT SLIPPED OFF."

Make sure the student is using enough chalk. Have the climber brush off the holds and try the moves again. If this continues to be a problem, the climber will need to work on contact strength (systems board and/or campus board) to increase strength on contact with the holds. If the climber is slipping off holds, it could also be a problem with body position on the wall, so balance and body tension need to be addressed.

"I'M NOT GOOD AT SLOPERS/CRIMPERS/ETC."

If a student has a gaping hole in a technique, she needs to work on whatever that specific flaw is until it becomes a strength. A climber having problems holding slopers needs to set up routes/boulder problems below her ability that use only slopers. This can be extremely frustrating to a climber who can easily climb 5.12 and you tell her to climb 5.11- sloper problems, especially if she is unable to complete the problems. The easiest response, however, is to point out the consequences: "If you encounter slopers on a 5.12 final route in a competition and you can do every other move except that one, then that will be your high point, even if it's the third move on the route." Make a weakness into a strength whenever one is identified.

"I CAN DO ALL THE MOVES, BUT I CAN'T FINISH THE ROUTE/PROBLEM."

This will indicate a slight lack of endurance. The climber needs to assess the rests and take full advantage of them so that she is fully recovered before reaching the part on the climb where she falls. By dividing the climb into sections and resting on a good hold between each section, she can gain confidence. After she does it in three sections, break it into two zones. Once that is mastered, she can try to red-point the route again. If it is still a problem, find out where she is falling and have her start four or five moves below that point and try to make it to the top. Once that is accomplished, she should start a few holds lower on each attempt until she can do it from the ground up without falling. Work endurance!

"I CAN DO THE MOVE AFTER I REST."

This is probably an endurance issue. To work endurance, see previous excuse and counterexcuse and see Chapter 12.

"IT'S TOO SCRUNCHY."

Tall climbers can get their feet so high that it is difficult to move from the position. Flexibility is one solution to this problem, because the more flexible a climber is, the easier it is to get in and out of cramped positions (see "Stretching" in Chapter 16). Another solution is to look around for other footholds that may make for a better body position. Sometimes routes are just scrunchy and the taller the climber, the worse the problem.

"MY SHOES DON'T STICK."

Body tension is probably the solution here. The shoes do not make the climber, and any climber who blames it on his rubber probably cannot see his own poor technique. Good exercises include "quiet feet" and any body tension exercises (see Chapter 5, Exercises to Work on Technique). The student needs to trust his shoes, but often when the technique improves, so will the trust.

"I'M OUT OF BALANCE."

This could be a good time to back down and work on basic balance techniques (see Chapter 5). Also make sure there are no footholds missing from the route and that the student sees all the footholds available. The climber can try different positions and watch other people on the climb to determine if everyone is out of balance, or just her. Some moves are simply awkward, but most moves in the gym are set up to be completed, so it could just be a matter of working the move in a different way.

"IT'S TOO REACHY."

This excuse can only be used in the worst possible route setting scenarios. Sometimes being short requires developing better footwork than a taller climber. Short climbers typically need to be more flexible so that they can get their feet higher on the wall. If a student believes a route is too reachy, she needs to look around for higher feet, smear, or find alternative positions to reach the next hold. Short climbers have to develop more dynamic movement than taller climbers so they can reach holds that are farther away. For this excuse, have the student concentrate on footwork and dynamic movement.

> At 5'1", Lynn Hill didn't use her height as an excuse; she learned how to use her feet more efficiently.

"IT WASN'T MY TYPE OF CLIMB."

This excuse tells you that the climber is not versatile enough. Have the climber write down that particular climb in his journal with the notation: "Work more on 'XX' type of climb." As the coach, you will need to have the climber spend the next few weeks working on only that type of climb until it becomes easier for him and not a hindrance. He will probably encounter that particular type of hold in a competition; so it cannot be a weakness and should be worked until it is a strength.

"I'M AN ENDURANCE CLIMBER AND IT WAS A POWERFUL CLIMB."

The next three to four weeks should be spent working just on power until it becomes a strength rather than a weakness.

"I'M A BOULDERER AND THAT WAS A LONG PROBLEM."

Even climbers who only boulder need some endurance. If a problem is twenty moves long and the boulderer only works problems under fifteen moves, he needs to have a little endurance to finish out a longer problem. Endurance will never *hurt* a boulderer, but the lack of endurance can definitely be a hindrance—especially if a boulderer is looking at a 20-foot fall because he can't squeak out the last two moves to the top.

Chapter 16: **Life Outside Climbing**

Injury Prevention and Treatment

"Pain is inevitable. Suffering is optional."
—Aaron Shamy

If a climber shows any signs of injury, make him stop climbing immediately—this does not mean climbing easy routes, it means the session is over. If a student ever hears a "pop" or feels pain in a finger, elbow, or shoulder, have him see a professional immediately and go to rehabilitation—tendons do not heal quickly. A torn tendon can take up to a year to heal completely. The climber may think he is better in a few weeks, but he will redamage the tendon if he climbs before it has started to heal. The injured area must be rested for at least two weeks, if not a month, then the climber can slowly build back up to using the injured area. There is no way to tape an injury tightly enough to use it for climbing; it is better to just tape it completely straight so that it cannot be used at all.

If there is pain in a tendon or muscle, ice it immediately. Freeze two parts water and one part rubbing alcohol in a Ziploc bag to make a "slushy" and cover the area completely to get deep into the tendon. Be sure to put a thin cloth, half a tissue, between the skin and the "slushy." It is colder than regular ice and can cause frostbite. Ice the area for twenty minutes and then off for thirty minutes. Repeat a minimum of three times during the first few hours after an injury. Icing the injury will bring down the swelling and help expedite healing. Injuries should be iced for approximately three days after the injury occurs, longer if the swelling continues. Anti-inflammatory, over-the-counter drugs (such as ibuprofen) can also help keep the swelling down and speed the healing time.

SLUSHY FORMULA:
2 cups water
1 cup rubbing alcohol
Freeze overnight in a Ziploc bag. Return to the freezer after each use.

Time Off

Encourage your students to take time off from climbing a few times a year. Two weeks is ideal to let the body recover from the stress it deals with during hard training cycles.

The big statement you can expect to hear from young climbers is "I'm young, I don't need time off." While this may be a somewhat valid argument, the fact is that by giving the body a break from climbing, the body will actually be stronger than before the time off. The reason is a somewhat surprising phenomenon: Once the body is given a chance to rest from a strenuous activity and then returns to the activity, the muscles will be in prime condition from the rest, and the body will typically remember the "good" engrams and not the bad. A climber who takes a two-week break should be able to come back at the same ability level as when he started the break.

Anything longer than a two-week break may require a little more work to get to the same place, but his climbing will progress at a quicker rate than before the break because the body is fully recovered and not compensating for fatigue or injury. If the climber has taken a month off from climbing, the first two weeks will be the most difficult because her ability level will be slightly lower than before the break. Fortunately, the body is able to remember climbing movement; as soon as the climber begins practicing regularly, her ability level will increase dramatically.

Encourage time off for a climber who is experiencing a plateau. After a two-week break, his ability should improve.

Growth Spurts

When working with kids, be aware that they may go through growth spurts while you are training them. If the student is continuously tired, a growth spurt may be coming on. Growing can cause a disruption in climbing, since the student may temporarily lose hand/eye coordination skills. This can be a problem from one week to the next in a few different ways. If a previously fluid climber is suddenly stumbling around on the wall, unsure of where to put his feet, it may be because he has lost the ability to determine the proximity of his feet and hands to the wall. The climber will have to adjust his climbing style for this change. Sometimes kids will tend to bring their feet too high when they have suffered a growth spurt, so they need to learn to extend the body more. Another important consideration is to make sure the kids are keeping their entire body fit and not overdeveloping in one area.

Stretching

Stretching is the best form of injury prevention. Have your student stretch a minimum of ten minutes after warming up to prevent pulling a muscle. Stretching the upper body is probably more important for climbing than stretching the lower body, but stretch the entire body. Climbers should stretch their forearms and fingers during the workout and also between climbs to keep the blood flowing through the muscles and keep the tendons supple. Stretching is a must to avoid stiff, sore muscles after a workout.

Maintaining flexibility is one of the most important aspects of a fitness routine. Stretching will help the climber maintain good posture and efficient movement and will reduce the risk of muscle and joint injury. In order to improve flexibility, climbers should stretch a minimum of four days per week, although stretching every day is ideal. Take each stretch to the point of discomfort (not pain) and hold for fifteen to thirty seconds. Repeat each stretch two to five times. Each time an area is stretched, it will become slightly more flexible.

With multiple students, you have the chance to do partnered stretching, working together to increase flexibility. For this type of stretching, someone will physically push the student into the stretch, pushing only to the point of resistance. It is important during partnered stretching that the person stretching communicates the point of pain so that she is not stretched to the point of injury.

If you are doing partnered stretching, one of the most beneficial ways to stretch is the three-part stretch. The climber initiates a stretch—for example, inner thigh, feet are together, knees open to the sides—and the partner pushes up on the climber's knees while the climber resists. After approximately five to ten seconds, the partner releases the pressure and the climber relaxes once again into the stretch. Repeat three to five times, taking the stretch farther each time.

Upper Body Stretches

Repeat each of the stretches below on both sides of the body.

FOREARM

Extend the right arm straight out in front of the body, palm down, and elbow slightly bent. With the left hand, pull the right hand toward the sky. Resist with the right hand and the muscles on the underside of the forearm will stretch. This stretch can also be done while resting on a route. With one hand on a rest hold, press the fingers of the opposite hand against the upper leg, pushing the palm away from the body with the wrist bent.

FOREARM (FRONT SIDE)

With the left arm extended in front of the body, elbow slightly bent, palm down, pull the palm toward the forearm with the right hand. To increase the stretch, curl the fingers toward the palm.

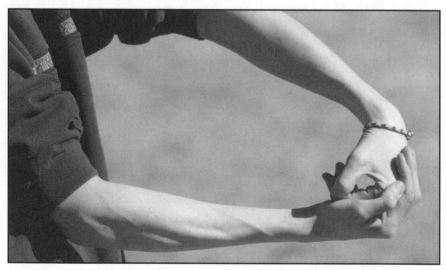

Forearm (front side): Curl the fingers of the left hand toward the palm to stretch out the forearm just a little more. Photo: Stewart Green

FINGERS

While there are no muscles in the fingers, there are tendons, which take a lot of abuse from climbing. It is important to have supple tendons in the fingers so that they will not tear easily. In order to increase the flexibility in the fingers, start this

Forearm: Stretching the fingers against the body while resting, with the palm facing away, can help dissipate lactic acid in the forearms. Photo: Stewart Green

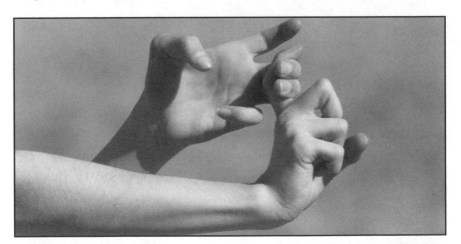

Fingers: Initiate the stretch of the right index finger with the first joint, cradling the tendons with the left hand. Finish the stretch by gently pulling back the tip of the right index finger. Photo: Stewart Green

stretch gently. Extend the right hand in front of the body, pointing the index finger straight up. Now take the middle two fingers of the left hand and cradle the first joint on the right index finger. Initiate the stretch by pulling the finger gently toward the body. Now take the index finger of the left hand and place it on the pad of the right index finger, stretching it gently until the finger is straight. Stretching gradually will keep the tendon from undertaking unnecessary stress. Repeat this stretch on each finger, then continue on the left hand.

Shoulders: Gently lower the body onto the arms, stretching the shoulders and back as the weight of the body presses down. Photo: Stewart Green

SHOULDER/BACK (WHILE LYING DOWN)

While lying flat on the stomach, push up onto the arms, arching the back. Now move the right arm to the left, under the torso, palm up. Gently lower the body onto the arm, stretching the back of the shoulders.

SHOULDER (WHILE LYING DOWN)

Still lying flat on the stomach, take the left arm straight out to the left. Push up on the right arm, rolling toward the left arm, and stretching the front of the arm/shoulder.

SHOULDER (WHILE STANDING/SITTING)

While sitting or standing, take the left arm across the torso, hugging it in close to the body with the right arm and making sure the shoulder is down and does not shrug or roll forward.

NECK

Sitting up straight, tilt the head to the left, ear to the shoulder, dropping the right shoulder toward the floor. To increase the stretch, push the right palm toward the floor (or hold on to the edge of a chair), dropping the shoulder even farther. If more of a stretch is desired, use the left hand to pull the head over even farther.

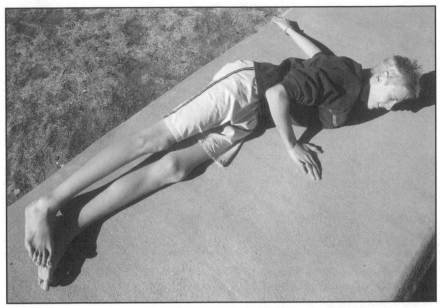

Shoulders: With the left arm behind the body, gently roll the shoulder skyward to stretch the front of the opposite shoulder. Photo: Stewart Green

Shoulders: Pulling the left arm across the body, hug it in close with the right arm to stretch out the left shoulder. Photo: Stewart Green

Neck: Proper positioning while stretching is key. To stretch out the neck, drop the shoulder down and pull the fingers upward. Photo: Stewart Green

ABDOMINALS (ON STOMACH)

While lying flat, face down, prop the upper body up on the hands. Arch the back and push the torso upward, stretching the head toward the ceiling, and keeping the pelvis and hips touching the floor.

Abs: Arch the back and let the abs stretch. Photo: Stewart Green

ABDOMINALS (ON BACK)

Lying flat on the back, stretch the arms straight overhead, with toes pointed in the opposite direction. Let the back arch, stretching the front of the stomach.

Lower Body Stretches

THE FROG (LYING DOWN)

Lying flat on the stomach, bring the knees up, out to the side, and press the feet into a wall. Press the hips into the ground. When done properly, the knees should be straight out to the side, forming a straight line from each knee through the hips. The feet should be positioned directly down from the knees, at a 90-degree angle. If the hips are off the floor, raise the upper body off the floor with the arms to press the hips farther into the floor. This will stretch the inner thighs or turnout, helping the climber to get his hips closer to the wall.

Turnout: For this stretch, make sure the knees and hips are in a straight line. Use a wall to keep the feet aligned, and press the hips downward and back toward the wall to stretch the inner thighs. Photo: Stewart Green

THE FROG (STANDING)

While standing, point the feet out to the sides and squat down, knees directly over the heels. The knees should be straight out to the side of the body, stretching the inner thighs. Place the hands on the knees to press them back one at a time to individually stretch each inner thigh. This stretch is also called a turnout, which refers to the flexibility of the hip joint and how far the knees can rotate to the outside of the body with knees bent.

HAMSTRINGS (STANDING)

With the feet close together, lean forward toward the ground, and let the weight of the upper body bring the torso close to the legs. Try to touch the floor with the hands. If this is not possible, cross one leg in front of the other and hug the legs in with the arms to stretch the backs of the legs. An added benefit of this exercise is stretching the lower back and shoulder muscles.

Hamstrings: Let the upper body roll downward to stretch the back of the legs. Photo: Stewart Green

HAMSTRINGS (SITTING)

While sitting on the floor, stretch the legs straight out in front of the body, and flex the feet so that the toes are pointing to the ceiling. Lean the body over the legs, toward the feet. If possible, grasp the feet and pull the body closer to the legs. You can also stretch one leg at a time by crossing one foot over the opposite knee and leaning forward. Another way to stretch the hamstrings is lying flat on the back with one leg against the floor without bending the knee. The other leg stretches straight up into the air, as close to the body as possible.

Hamstrings: As the climber stretches toward the toes with the upper body, the coach can gently press on the back to help increase the stretch. Photo: Stewart Green

Hip flexor: To stretch the front of the leg, sit up tall and push the hips forward. Photo: Stewart Green

HIP FLEXOR

Bend down so that the right knee is on the ground, the right leg extended behind the body, and the weight of the body straight up from the right knee. The upper left leg extends straight in front of the body, the foot flat on the ground and the left knee directly over the ankle. Tilt the hips forward and lift the chest up, pushing forward through the front of the right leg to feel a stretch through the hip flexor— the area directly below the hip bone and pelvis. Hold for twenty to thirty seconds. Another way to stretch the hip flexor is on a bench with one leg hanging off the end of the bench at the knee. Pull the opposite knee in close to the body, stretching the hip flexor of the opposite leg.

CALVES (STANDING AGAINST A WALL)

Facing a wall, take the feet approximately 3 feet away from the wall but still together, and keep the hands on the wall. With the legs straight, lean into the wall, keeping the heels on the floor. If enough of a stretch is not felt through the calves (lower legs), take the legs farther out from the wall. To stretch each calf individually, cross the left foot over the right ankle and put more pressure on the right leg, stretching closer to the wall.

Calves: Lean forward into the wall to stretch out the back of the leg. By crossing over the opposite foot, more pressure is put on the standing leg, thus increasing the stretch.
Photo: Stewart Green

GLUTEUS MAXIMUS/HIPS (STANDING WITH LEG CROSSED)

Stand on the left leg and cross the right foot above the left knee. Sit back into the right hip, pushing with most of the body weight.

Gluteus maximus: Push back into the hip of the crossed leg to get a stretch through the back of the leg and buttocks.
Photo: Stewart Green

GLUTEUS MAXIMUS/HIPS (SITTING WITH ONE LEG STRAIGHT OUT)

While sitting on the floor, keep the left leg straight out and cross the right foot over the left knee. Press the body forward, into the legs to stretch the right hip. Another great hamstring stretch is done while lying flat on the back: Cross the right foot over the left knee, then roll the hips in until the hands can wrap around the left thigh, bringing both legs to the chest.

Gluteus maximus: Cross the leg above the knee to stretch the back of the straight leg and the buttocks on the bent leg. A partner can help increase this stretch by pressing gently on the student's back. Photo: Stewart Green

INNER THIGHS (LEGS APART)

Sit on the floor with the legs spread apart in a "V." Flex the feet so that the toes are pointing upward to the ceiling. Lean the body forward, toward the floor, and try to get the torso as close to the floor as possible.

Inner thighs: With the legs spread as wide as possible, the student leans forward. The ultimate goal is to touch the stomach to the floor. Photo: Stewart Green

OBLIQUES (LEGS APART/SITTING)

With the legs spread apart on the floor, feet flexed, lean the body over the left leg, torso facing sideways. Take the right arm over the body toward the left foot, stretching the outer abdominals. Now turn and face the leg, stretching both hands toward the foot.

Inner thighs and obliques: Turn the upper body to face the leg to stretch out the side of the torso. Photo: Stewart Green

Weight Training

The jury is out on whether weight training can benefit climbing. Personally I believe that the better physical condition a person is in the better she will climb, but that doesn't necessarily mean adding muscular bulk. Maintaining good muscular strength will help the student perform activities without fatigue, residual soreness, or risk of injury.

One important thing to remember is that young bodies are still in a developmental state and overworking the muscles with weight training can damage the body structure. Care must be taken if a young climber decides to take up weight training.

Climbing works nearly every muscle in the body, so most muscles are worked enough that they don't need extra weight training. There are a few muscles that do not get developed while climbing, however, and those are the ones that should to be worked to prevent an "imbalance." For example, if the biceps are overdeveloped from climbing and the triceps are not sufficiently developed, an imbalance can create an elbow problem.

The areas that can be worked outside climbing are the triceps, the back (posture), the legs, and the abdominals. These areas can be worked at home or in a health club. If a climber wants to embark on an entire weight training regiment, her climbing ability can benefit. The results will most likely be seen in overall strength and endurance. The two basic ways to work muscular strength are endurance training and strength training. Have your student speak with a personal trainer to develop a weightlifting program.

Be sure your student stretches the muscles he is using during climbing and weight training to keep them elongated. If those muscles do not get stretched, they can become shortened, and the climber will not have full range of motion or power with them.

Strength training will build muscular bulk, which can be a downside. Because muscles weigh more than fat, the scale may show an increase. As long as the increase is due to heavier muscles, it is not a problem; the benefit of being stronger can outweigh the downside of carrying more mass up the rock. There is a fine line, however, between gaining muscle and gaining power. Too much bulk can hinder the climber, so the climber needs to decide whether weight training will help him become a better climber.

Another method of weight training is to use light weights with a lot of repetition. This will develop muscular endurance rather than bulk. In this method, your student would have a weight that is easy to lift and do twelve to fifteen repetitions. She should rest for a minute and then do twelve to fifteen more repetitions. Three sets of weights with each muscle group are necessary for endurance training. Weights should not be lifted to the point of failure in a muscular-endurance program.

Aerobic Conditioning

While climbing is not considered an aerobic sport, training the lung capacity is beneficial, especially for endurance training and recovery. Building up an aerobic base will help a climber of any ability. The ability to breathe and have muscular recovery depends on the capability of the body to utilize its oxygen intake, and aerobic fitness will define the student's capacity to sustain long periods of muscular activity. This is beneficial because less effort will be exerted, and the climber will retain a larger reserve for emergency situations.

When climbing at a top level, there are very few places on hard routes to actually stop, rest, breathe, and recover. Therefore, the better conditioned the athlete is, the easier it will be to recover while climbing.

To build up a healthy aerobic base, climbers can participate in many activities, such as bicycle riding, step aerobics, dance, running, walking, and hiking. These activities should be performed at least four days per week for a minimum of thirty minutes per day.

(*Note:* Climbing may not be an aerobic sport—the heart rate does not get into the 75 to 85 percent aerobic training range—but the heart rate does increase to the fat-burning range, which is around 60 percent of maximum heart rate.)

Cross Training

There is no doubt that cross training can vastly improve climbing performance. Cross training not only means aerobic conditioning such as biking, running, or other sports but also being versatile in climbing. Every climber has a favorite type of climbing, and it is easy to become specialized in one or two activities while the rest of his abilities do not improve. A boulderer should work endurance, a slab climber may want to get on overhangs, and an endurance climber will need to boulder and build some power. Cross training is essential, whether it is training cardiovascular fitness to improve endurance or bouldering to improve power for onsighting. The key is to recognize weaknesses and then choose a form of cross training that will help improve those areas.

Chapter 17: **Let's Go Climbing!**

Let's face it, this entire book has been the prelude for the main objective, right? The kids have been begging you to take them climbing outside, and now is your chance to gain a little knowledge for that exhilarating day. Most kids who climb in a gym really want to climb outside—do some "real" climbing—out in the elements, on natural rock. Believe it or not, I have met some young climbers who have never climbed outside but have spent 100 percent of their time climbing

Warming up in Fern Canyon, outside Boulder, Colorado.
Photo: Rod Willard

indoors, and it's not from lack of trying! Usually climbing indoors is a huge convenience for everyone—climbers, parents, and instructors—so the chance to climb outside is put off. For an old-time climber—one who started climbing before there were gyms—this is shocking. I started climbing outdoors and can't imagine climbing only indoors.

A few students may not want to climb outdoors, and that is fine. Climbing indoors has become a sport in itself, and although climbing on natural rock will help build a climber's repertoire, it is not for everyone.

This chapter is not designed to teach you how to climb outdoors. Rather it points at the differences between indoor gym climbing and outdoor climbing, along with references of where to get the information you need to set up outdoor climbs.

My first piece of advice is to get a professional instructor to take you outside—and become a *safety fanatic* before ever taking out your students. Make sure you have proper training in first-aid skills so that if something does happen while the kids are in your care, you can take care of them.

If you have never climbed outside but already know how to climb from being in an indoor gym, getting on real rock for the first time can be a bit intimidating. Let's start at the beginning and assume, because you are coaching kids in a climbing gym, that you will be starting with either toprope or sport climbs.

Liability

When you decide to take your students into the world of outdoor climbing, you will be accepting a huge liability and must have the proper insurance. Make sure you have the parents sign waivers for their minor children and that you have covered yourself. Remember, though, a waiver might not stand up in court. Climbing is considered by some to be a dangerous activity, especially insurance companies, and an accident may not be covered—even if it is not your fault. If you are coaching through another organization, such as a school, you will also need to find out what paperwork is required for you to take your students outdoors.

Some climbing gyms may have an outdoor climbing program already in place, but double- and triple-check that you are personally covered under the gym's policy. If you are doing this as a "fun" activity and it is not associated with a certified guide service, you will undeniably want to have the parents accompany you—each and every time—for liability's sake.

The Difference

While it is true that the techniques learned in a gym do cross over to climbing outside, there are also some major differences. Some differences are obvious and
some are not. The first thing you will probably notice when you get to the base of
a climb is the quality of the air. Ah—take a deep breath and notice how you don't
inhale a lung full of chalk dust. The crags are typically not as crowded as a gym,
although some areas are extremely popular and you may have to wait for a
climb—especially for easier routes.

**Michelle Hurni stemming on the tufa on Cayman Brac.
You won't find this wall in the gym!** Photo: Skip Harper

The biggest difference in climbing the great outdoors versus the controlled
indoors is the safety factor. Indoors you are using ropes that belong to someone
else, draws that are prehung, and topropes that are already hanging. Basically you
can go into a gym and just climb. Going to the crag means more work on everyone's part. There's the extra gear, the setup, the hike in, locating the climbs, and
many other factors that are not an issue when you walk into a gym and pay your
entrance fee.

One of the factors a first-time outdoor climber will notice is how blank the rock looks. Sure, there are contours, lines, cracks, etc., but a gym climber may not know how to interpret these things using their indoor brain.

There is absolutely no tape that marks the way to the top. Even guidebooks for a given area sometimes give ambiguous directions: "This climb begins at the bottom of a left-leaning oak tree." What? How long ago was this book written? Is this dead tree the same "left-leaning oak?" Climbing outdoors is a different world, and it will take some getting used to.

Along the same lines, without tape how does the climber know which holds can be used and which ones are considered out of bounds? Typically a guidebook will give some instructions about where the climb begins and where the climb ends. It's even easier if it's a sport climb where you can follow the bolts to the top. A guidebook may also let you know if the "huge ledge with the bird's nest" is in or out of bounds.

Holds come in many shapes and sizes, and the only way to know what is coming up is actually to climb on the rock itself. Sandstone feels gritty and is usually not too sharp. Limestone can be rounded and feel slick. Granite is typically pink or gray and can have sharp edges and crystals. Most people develop a personal preference for one type of rock or another. I prefer sandstone, even though I know the rock can be less stable than limestone.

Remember, any new area you go to will take some time to get used to, just like going to unfamiliar gyms with different angles, holds, and route setters. Ratings can feel different, route finding can be complicated—and the rock can chew up your skin and spit it out.

Some people find climbing outside easier than climbing inside. The reason for this is that there are sometimes more options for the hands and feet. You don't have to depend on where the route setter placed the blue tape; you can use any holds that are available. This can make it more straightforward for a shorter climber who doesn't have to depend on the exact location of holds on an indoor wall but can use whichever holds he can reach.

On that same note, climbing outside can seem more challenging to other climbers. With no tape to guide the way to the top of the climb, the climber must think for herself and figure out which holds to use. If you climb in an area that is not heavily populated, there may not be chalk on the holds to point the way. The footholds may seem miniscule, especially when they are not marked, and seem difficult to trust. It can be daunting to read the route from the bottom and decide which holds to use. A route where you don't know the holds may take longer to climb as you hang out and determine the sequence while on the rock.

The bolts in place for leading an outdoor sport route are basically the same as in a gym but will probably be farther apart outdoors. Bolts and bolt hangers are placed with either a hand drill or a power drill, whereas in the gym they are attached to the plywood and then anchored behind the wall for safety. For more information on the history of bolts and proper bolt placement, *Climbing Anchors* by John Long (part of the How to Climb! series) is an excellent reference.

Belaying

Belaying outdoors for a lead climb is different from belaying in the gym, where the bolts are probably closer together. Make sure you get proper belay instruction for belaying outside; while the fundamentals are the same indoors and out, there are many differences that only a seasoned outdoor climber can teach you.

The Elements

Many factors come into play when climbing outdoors that are never even a consideration when training in the gym. The weather is the first and foremost factor to consider when venturing to the crags. Some climbing areas are remote, and you will have to hike to get to the base of the climbs. In this case, make sure you check the weather forecast. Think about being an hour from the car when a lightening storm comes up. Dangerous? Darned right, especially with all that metal climbers carry on their body. Sure, you can carry rain gear and be "prepared," but what if you are on a multipitch climb 200 feet above the ground with 100 feet more to the top, and then the hike out? Always consider Mother Nature when on a climbing adventure. Check the weather report—and take extra clothing just in case.

> Some areas have other natural hazards, such as the flying, slithering, and walking kinds. I once stuck my hand into a crack at The Beehive at Stoney Point, California, dislodged an entire swarm of bees, and discovered the hard way that the crag was appropriately named. Rumors fly about climbers at the Red River Gorge, Kentucky, who fall off routes when snakes are dislodged from the slopes above and land on them. Climbers beware: There are plenty of obstacles to overcome—and not all include the crux!

In sport climbing and toproping, there can be a hike to the crags. Don't forget any of your gear in the car when you leave on that forty-five-minute hike! Be sure the shoes you are wearing will work for the hike in, especially with the extra weight of gear and ropes on your back. The pack you choose should be comfortable and not rub on the shoulders. Take a snack and plenty of water, too.

When climbing in a 40-foot climbing gym, there may be a bit of noise, but generally communication is not a problem. Outdoors, however, wind can create a challenge, making it difficult for the belayer to understand the climber and vice versa. It is vital to make a plan before the climber leaves the ground. The belayer and climber must both know how the climber plans to get down from the top of the climb. Will the climber be walking off the top? Will she be threading the rope through the anchor and lowering herself off, rappelling? Maybe he will thread the anchor and be lowered off by the belayer. Will he expect to be lowered by the belayer without any change to the anchor? In a gym there is no question, but outdoors there are plenty—all of which can be extremely serious if misunderstood.

> Bobbi Bensman (once one of the top female climbers in the United States) was dropped from the top of a climb at Rifle, Colorado, when her belayer thought she said "off belay." What she really said was "okay," and she expected her belayer to take up the slack in the rope and lower her off the climb. Hitting some tree branches on the way down broke her fall, but she could have been seriously injured because of a miscommunication. Whether on toprope or leading, make communication a top priority.

Climbing Etiquette

Climbing outside in the great outdoors requires some etiquette to keep things safe and fun for everyone. By following the rules listed below, everyone can have a good time.

- If you see someone doing something dangerous, be courteous but let them know.

- If someone is on the climb you want to get on, find out if anyone else is waiting. If there is no one else in front of you, you can lay out your rope to stake your claim. Be patient, especially if it looks as though the party in front of you is going to be awhile. Remember, he was there first.

- If you are going to be on a climb for a significant amount of time, let those waiting know so that they can decide to wait for the climb or make other plans.

- If you are working a route—taking multiple laps—you can always let someone else climb on your rope or draws while you are resting. This can help alleviate tension if other climbers are getting impatient.

- If there is a climb that already has quick draws hanging and you want to climb it, find out whose draws they are and get permission from the owner before you climb on them.

- Keep your pets under control if there are other people around. Don't let your dog walk on other people's gear.

- Don't distract other climbers or belayers. Too much chatter can be dangerous when signals are being exchanged.

Is This Toprope Safe?

There are many aspects to consider when you climb outside. If done properly, it is not much different from climbing indoors. *Toproping*, by Peter Lewis, part of the How to Climb series, is a great source for learning how to set up topropes safely. Refer to *Toproping* for detailed information before you climb or set up topropes outside.

Bolts

On a sport climb, there will be bolts and bolt hangers leading the way to the top and then anchors for lowering off the top of the climb. Typically the bolts and anchors are installed by an unknown person, although sometimes the guidebook will inform you. Check out *Climbing Anchors* by John Long for details on how bolts are placed and other information on using fixed protection.

Following are a few safety considerations that you can look for at a sport climbing area:

- Do the bolts come out of the rock or wiggle? *Bolts and bolt hangers should not be loose.*

- Do the bolt hangers spin on the bolts? *Bolt hangers should be flush and snug against the rock.*

- Are the bolts going straight into the rock, or are they at an angle? *The bolt should go straight into the rock, with the bolt hanger flat against the rock without any space showing around it.*

- Are the bolt hangers deformed? *A bolt hanger on the rock should be in the same condition as a brand-new one. If there are visible deep scratches in the bolt or bolt hanger, or if it is bent, the strength of the metal has been compromised and it should not be climbed on.*

- Are there cracks or rust on the bolts or bolt hangers? *In some areas, bolts can become corroded and/or rusted, which makes the metal weaker. Make sure the bolt and bolt hangers do not look damaged.*

- Are the bolt hangers homemade, or are there ¼" bolts? *Some older climbs may have homemade hangers (common at Shelf Road in Colorado) or ¼" bolts, and they are probably not as strong as manufactured equipment.*

- Are there anchors at the top of the climb? *You don't want to get to the top of a climb and find out there are no anchors. If you can see the top of the climb, make sure there is a way to lower off! If you cannot, evaluate how you will get down.*

- Are the anchors intact? *Before leaving the ground, determine to the best of your ability if the bolt hangers and anchors are all in place and not chopped or bent.*

If any of these factors are even the slightest bit questionable, do not climb that route! Other factors can make a bolt suspicious, so pay careful attention and ask around. Most areas are bolted by only a few people—it is a lot of work—and they usually know what they are doing, but if there are questionable routes take the time to do your research before climbing—or don't climb at that cliff.

One scary aspect when climbing outside is not being able to see all the bolts before leaving the ground. Sometimes there is a note in the guidebook that tells you how many draws to take with you, which is extremely helpful but may not be accurate. Take extras!

I once took the exact number of quick draws listed in the guidebook. Finding myself two bolts from the top with no more quick draws on my harness taught me a huge lesson. Now I always take extras.

Another consideration is whether the climb is 100 percent bolted sport or whether it has some bolts and also requires some traditional gear. If a sport climb follows a crack for part of the way, most traditional climbers will not put a bolt where a piece of removable gear—camalot, nut, hex—could be easily inserted. Make sure you know this vital piece of information before leaving the ground. If you do not see a bolt where you think there should be one, you may need removable gear.

Clipping Bolts

Although clipping the rope through the quick draws outdoors is the same as in the gym, outdoors you will have to clip the draws to the bolt hangers because they are not permanently hung as they are in the gym. *Advanced Rock Climbing* by John Long and Craig Leubben has an entire chapter on sport climbing, including clipping quick draws.

Arranging the draws ahead of time makes it easy to find them when the time comes. Photo: Rod Willard

A few things to think about when sport climbing outside that don't come into play in a gym include the following:

1. Before leaving the ground, make sure you have the proper number of quick draws—along with two for the anchors and a few extras.

2. Arrange the quick draws on your harness so that you can easily reach them. I usually distribute them evenly on each side, unless I know that all the draws are clipped with one hand. In this case, I will put most of the quick draws on that side.

3. For safety reasons, use a quick draw with one locking carabiner on the first bolt hanger to ensure that the rope will not come unclipped for any reason.

4. If you are using bent gate and straight gate carabiners, the straight gate goes in the bolt hanger and the rope goes through the bent gate carabiner. It is easier to clip the rope into a bent gate than a straight gate.

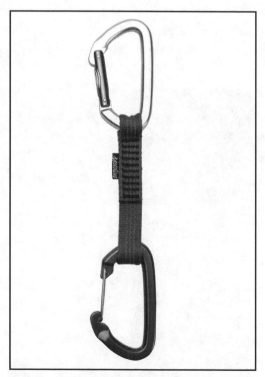

Always put the straight gate carabiner in the bolt hanger, with the bent gate or wire gate at the bottom of the quick draw for the rope to run through. Photo: Metolius

5. Get into a good solid stance before clipping the bolt, take a deep breath, clip the quick draw into the bolt hanger, and then clip the rope into the quick draw.

6. Try not to clip above the head—always clip at head level or below. Remember, if you pull up a lot of rope and come off, you will fall farther than if you are clipping at waist level.

7. Communicate with your belayer so that you have the slack you need for clipping.

8. Know what a "Z" clip is—and avoid doing it at all costs.

9. To avoid a backclip, make sure the rope runs from the rock face through the quick draw to the climbing harness. If the rope is running toward the rock through the quick draw, it can come unclipped if the climber takes a fall above the draw.

10. Don't let the rope run behind your leg; keep it in front or to the side of the body at all times.

Topping Out

TOPROPE (TR)

When you get to the top of a climb, there are many ways to get down. The quickest way down on toprope is to be lowered without any modifications to the anchors. This is the same as in a climbing gym—communicate with your belayer, feel the rope come taut, and then sit back for the ride down. Read *Toproping* by Peter Lewis for more information on lowering off a climb.

"Topping out" is also an option. This is climbing above the anchor a safe distance from the edge with the intent of walking down the backside of the climb. For this option, the climber must step back away from the edge of the cliff, untie the rope from her harness, pull up enough rope to reach the ground, and then toss the rope to the ground for the next climber—all without taking the rope out of the top anchors. At this point, the climber must find a way back to the base of the climb. Never top out unless you know the way down.

When using a toprope outdoors, someone must eventually disassemble the TR setup. Usually the last person on the route will top out, take down all the gear, and then hike back to the base of the climb. Stay back away from the edge of the climb, and be careful not to step on any ropes or gear lying on the ground; it's easy to stumble and take a long fall to the ground. For safety reasons, if at all possible, tie into a tree away from the edge of the climb while removing the TR anchors.

SPORT CLIMBING

With sport climbing, whether you are "seconding" or "following" (both terms mean climbing to the top of a sport climb on toprope) or leading, there are numerous ways to get down. Usually sport climbs end before the top of the rock wall, so it is not possible to "top out" and walk off the top. There should be at least two anchors at the top of the sport climb, and these anchors can vary in style.

The easiest anchors to use are cold shuts, which are a "J"- or hook-shaped piece of metal. Some are angled enough so that the rope will not come out; others have a snap lock on the top so that the rope is absolutely secure and can't jiggle out. With cold shuts, all the climber has to do is place the rope across both anchors and get lowered down; there is no gear to remove or knots to untie.

If other climbers will be using the climb as a toprope, the leader should clip quick draws into the cold shuts so that the rope will run through the quick draws—not the cold shuts. Using quick draws on the cold shuts will save wear and tear on the anchor and rope. In this case, the final climber will have to switch the rope from the quick draws to the cold shuts to be lowered.

Another type of sport climbing anchor is a bolt hanger—the same as used on the route. Bolt hangers at the top of climbs can be the same size as on the route or larger and thicker, called rap hangers. Reference *Sport Climbing* by John Long for detailed instructions on lowering off a climb with bolt hangers.

CLEANING THE SPORT CLIMB

After cleaning up the anchor (refer to *Sport Climbing*), the climber is now lowered toward the ground by the belayer. On the way down the face of the climb, the climber removes all quick draws from the climb and clips them into the gear loops on his harness. This is easily done on a vertical climb, but it can be a bit more challenging on an overhanging or wandering climb.

If a climb is overhanging, the climber can use one of the spare quick draws from the anchor by attaching one carabiner of the quick draw into her belay loop and the other carabiner of the quick draw to the rope closest to the rock face. As

Cleaning steep routes can be a challenge, unless the climber is attached to the rope closest to the wall with a quick draw to keep him from swinging away from the wall. Photo: Stewart Green

the climber is lowered, this quick draw keeps the climber close to the rock face so that the other quick draws can be easily removed. On an overhanging climb, when the last quick draw—the one closest to the ground—is removed, there will be excessive slack in the system (sometimes enough to swing and/or hit the ground). In this case, the climber should either be spotted or skip it on the way down and then climb from the ground up to the first draw to remove it.

Exposure

You've probably heard the phrase "it was really exposed" and may not know what it means. "Exposure" is basically a quick-and-easy term that means being way off the deck (ground) with a sheer rock face in front of you and no sign of the top or a ledge in sight. Some people are never bothered by "exposure," while others freak out. My advice? Don't look down if you know you are going to freak out. This fear of heights can happen both on TR and on lead.

Ratings

Climbing outside and climbing in the gym can seem like different worlds, especially when you look at the numbers. In Chapter 1, I gave a list of ratings for climbs.

Most gyms and outdoor areas follow the Yosemite Decimal System, but the ratings can seem as though they don't even compare. Some areas are "soft" (the ratings are higher than the climb is hard), some are "sandbagged" (the ratings are easier and the climbs feel harder), and some feel harder or easier just because of the type of rock or style of climbing.

The Well-Rounded Climber

Climbing exclusively in one area can make it easy to advance through the ratings, but it doesn't necessarily make you a better climber. Make sure you and your students travel around to different types of rock and try out different styles of climbing: sport, traditional, and bouldering. Just like with training inside, make sure you and your students become proficient at crimpers, slopers, overhangs, and slabs. When climbing outside, there is usually a variety available in any given area.

Toprope versus Sport versus Trad versus Bouldering

Another consideration regarding the difficulty rating of climbs is whether you are toproping, leading a sport climb, or leading on traditional gear. With each type of climbing, the rating will feel a bit more demanding. Imagine, for instance, you are toproping a climb. There is no stopping for clipping, and you can continue to the top without that extra ten to sixty seconds that it takes to clip a quick draw into a bolt hanger and place the rope into the carabiner. In sport climbing those ten to sixty extra seconds can really add to the difficulty of the climb.

The next level of climbing is traditional (trad) climbing. In trad climbing the climber must figure out which piece of gear will fit into the crack, often trying a couple before getting it right. The correct length of runner (either a sewn quick draw or a tied piece of webbing) will then have to be clipped onto the gear and then the rope clipped into the runner. Whew—it can be extremely strenuous, and the proper placement of that gear is critical.

Bouldering is the sport that brings climbing to the most basic level: no ropes, no harness—only shoes, chalk, and a crash (landing) pad. Boulderers tend to have their own niche within the climbing community and typically do not tie into a rope—some infrequently and some never. You will see boulderers hanging around in groups at the base of large, freestanding rocks with large crash pads to soften

High off the deck, Shena Sturman has a spot pad, but where are her spotters? Photo: John Sherman

the fall when they come off problem. The joy of bouldering comes from being outside with a group of friends encouraging one another to try a problem or even just one move on a problem.

The biggest safety considerations for bouldering are to make sure there is plenty of protection at the base of each problem and to have spotters on all problems, especially if the problem is highball—topping out high off the ground.

As I am writing this book, the phone calls arrive, and with them the confirmation that another climbing friend is gone: one of the safest climbing partners any of us ever had—the one who always encouraged us to put in one more piece of protection, to double-check the anchor before lowering off, to stand as close to the rock face as possible when belaying. An unavoidable accident took him away from us too soon. We all accept the risk every time we step up to the base of a climb. No matter how safe we are, the risk is inherent. God be with you, Rod Willard—climbing partner and friend.

Guidebooks

There are books written for nearly every climbing area in the world. Guidebooks tell you the local ethics, any special concerns, rules, the local rating system, and closures. Some areas close certain routes during the season for animal breeding, nesting, and endangered species—plant and/or animal. Pay special attention to closures mentioned in the guidebooks, ask the locals, and check for special fliers posted in the parking areas.

Guidebooks vary but generally list the climbs, ratings, names, who did the first ascent, how many bolts are on sport routes, what type of gear you need for trad routes, if you need an extra-long rope, the descent, the type of rock, map of the area, topo of the climbs, and other helpful information. When looking at guidebooks, remember that they are not all created equal—some are great, some are not. Some guidebooks give very vague descriptions of climbs with inaccurate topographical maps; others are very reliable, detailed, and specific. There are sometimes updates available if an area has changed since the publication date. Check with your local climbing shops for any new information.

Additional Gear for Climbing Outdoors

The equipment used in the gym—shoes, harness, chalk bag, and belay device—will also be used when climbing outside, but the list of required items for outdoor climbing expands significantly, whether you are toproping or sport climbing. Since your student is most likely coming from climbing in a gym, I will not be discussing traditional climbing but sticking with the more familiar sport climbing. Please be advised that to trad climb, you will need extensive training in gear placement and other safety aspects. For more information on gear needed for toproping, sport climbing, or traditional climbing, read *Advanced Rock Climbing* by John Long and Craig Luebben.

ROPE

The first major item to add to the equipment list is a rope. A rope that has a little bit of stretch—dynamic—is a must. The most basic version of dynamic rope will set you back at least $100 for a 50-meter rope, but a 55-meter rope is more practical for most areas. For longer climbs, consider spending a little extra money for a 60-meter rope. When toproping and sport climbing, if you are getting lowered off the climbs, you have only half the length of the rope for the actual climb.

There are numerous other decisions to be made when purchasing a rope, and I suggest researching catalogs and asking friends to figure out what type of rope will best meet your needs.

"Dry" ropes are treated for wet conditions so that they do not get heavy when wet. Some ropes change color at the midway point, which indicates when you have reached halfway on the rope, but this feature adds to the overall cost. A rope's thickness also affects the strength and weight of the rope. Most companies offer ropes from 9 to 11 millimeters that can be used for both toproping and sport climbing. Sterling and Mammut are good choices for dynamic ropes.

When using your rope outside, make sure it is situated on a bag or tarp at the base of any climb to keep dirt off it. One of my favorite accessories is the Metolius Ropemaster. This bag is designed for carrying, storing, and laying (flaking) out the rope. A rope should never be stepped on by humans or animals, because grinding dirt into the core of the rope can damage it.

PROTECTION

For toprope climbing, webbing, locking carabiners, and quick draws with carabiners are necessary. The amount of webbing and protection to set up a toprope will depend on where you are climbing. Check your local guidebooks for the beta.

A basic sport climbing rack includes several quick draws that are a variety of lengths. Metolius sells preassembled quick draws, complete with a bent gate carabiner on one end for the rope and a straight gate on the other for clipping into the bolt hanger. Most sport climbs are not excessively long, and you can probably start with around twelve to fifteen quick draws.

HELMET

Climbing outdoors can sometimes be dangerous due to rock fall from above, and a helmet should always be worn when climbing outside. At sport climbing and bouldering areas, you will see climbers not wearing helmets, but do not let them influence you. Wearing a helmet can be a matter of life or death.

CRASH PAD

When bouldering outside, a crash pad is a necessity. Numerous companies currently produce "spot" pads—a foam pad used to protect a boulderer from hitting rocks or solid ground when falling from a problem. My favorite crash pad is from Metolius, and is available in sizes from 36" x 32" to 48" x 72". Most crash pads come with handles and shoulder straps so that you can carry them like a backpack. Shove your shoes and chalk bag into the center and you are set for a day outdoors!

STICK CLIP

Another item that can come in handy is a "stick clip." This stick is used to clip the first quick draw onto the first bolt on a sport climb while standing on the ground. This is done to prevent an accident if the climber were to come off the rock before the first clip is made.

Stick clips can be as primitive as a piece of wood found at the base of the climb, or as high tech as a kite-flying pole—an extension rod used for raising a large kite into the air. While frowned upon by some, especially more traditional climbers, it's better to be safe than sorry.

On the top end of the stick you will need something to hold a carabiner. A piece of white athletic tape can be used to hold the carabiner onto the stick, and another small piece can be used to hold the gate open. Other options can be found in the local hardware store. Plastic "stick clip" pieces are also available at climbing shops, which make stick clipping a cinch.

To use a stick clip, attach a quick draw to the top of the pole with the rope running through the bottom carabiner of the quick draw. The stick is then raised up and the top carabiner is hooked into the bolt hanger. Once the carabiner is hooked, the stick—tape and all—is jerked back so that the carabiner gate closes. The worst part about using a stick clip is that sometimes the tape will stay on the carabiner and hold the gate open. This is not an optimal situation, as the carabiner is not as strong with an open gate and could "dance" out of the bolt hanger. Try to get the gate to close *before* climbing up to the first quick draw.

Have Fun

The real reason anyone climbs outside is to have a good time in a natural setting. You will be instrumental in helping your students learn about climbing outdoors and having a good time—all while teaching safety as the fundamental standard.

Chapter 18: **Sponsorship**

Who Can Get Sponsored?

"The world will expect you to accomplish something BEFORE you feel good about yourself."
—Bill Gates

Anyone can get sponsored, but the important thing about sponsorship is making sure there is merit behind that support. Sponsorship is not just about getting free gear or equipment, it is about a mutual partnership between the climber or team and the company offering the contract for sponsorship. It takes a lot of work to get a sponsor and then make that sponsor happy.

Some companies will not sponsor climbers under the age of sixteen because the goals and ideals of young climbers change frequently. A climber may begin climbing strong and competing well, but he may tire of it in a year, leaving the investment the company has made in the climber a worthless one.

The main thing to remember about sponsorship is that the company comes first. The sponsoring company is doing the climber a favor by sponsoring her, and not the other way around. Make sure your climbers understand that small but vitally important fact.

Team Sponsorship

It can be beneficial for your students to form a team to gain sponsorship. When looking for team sponsorship, you will need to approach companies that will benefit by sponsoring your team. Sometimes local companies are willing to take on a team, create a uniform, donate some money for travel, or even provide transportation for the team to get to competitions.

Research the company before making contact so that the sponsorship becomes a long-term relationship and mutually beneficial. Talk to the company and make sure you understand what it expects from the team. Some companies may want a team photo, help with advertisements, or a special belay session for employees. The team should have something viable to offer in exchange for whatever the company is offering—in addition to a good attitude.

What should you expect from the company? That depends on what type of company it is. If it is a climbing shoe company, you can either expect discounted, maybe even free, shoes for your team members. This does not mean a lifetime or unlimited supply of shoes, but maybe just one pair for the sponsored climber and not his entire family. If the company is not climbing related, it might be able to offset coaching fees or provide team uniforms. Work with the company and find a solution that works for everyone.

Individual Sponsorship

Personally, I feel that a climber should not even try to get sponsored until he has climbed hard for a minimum of three years. This will prove to the sponsor that the climber is in it for more than free equipment. When I started climbing, I paid full retail for every piece of gear that I used for the first ten years. Climbing companies want to be promoted, but they are in the business of selling the equipment they manufacture, not giving it away.

Young climbers need to prove themselves in more than just one aspect of climbing in order to get a sponsor. They must have something to offer the company: exposure in magazines, publicity at top competitions, volunteering in the community, etc. Companies want maximum exposure, and that goes beyond wearing their shoes to the local climbing gym.

Sponsorship is a two-way street, and the climber should have the ultimate respect for any company she is approaching for a sponsorship. Companies receive hundreds of letters every week from climbers and competitions asking for sponsorship. The letter your climber writes should include something special that she can offer to the company—something that makes her stand out from the rest.

If the climber is only competing, he definitely needs another way to stand out, especially if he is not climbing very hard outside. The same goes for someone who is only bouldering/climbing outside and not participating in competitions. Either the climber needs to do both, or he must completely stand out in one or the other area. The climber should also be involved in other areas: maybe helping coach a young kids' program, participating in a special cleanup project at a local crag, or writing articles for one of the magazines. Unless your climber is the best in the country, sponsorship is not *just* about climbing but also about contributing to the climbing community.

Once the climber is sponsored, she should stick with that company and not switch around on a whim. Companies that see a climber switching companies or badmouthing a sponsor will probably not want to sponsor that climber in the future.

Sample Letter Tips

This letter should be written by the coach if it is for a team sponsorship and by the individual climber if it is for personal sponsorship.

- When writing a sponsorship letter to a company, make it as professional as possible. Try not to brag, unless it is something the climber is doing to better the climbing community. Be modest, but make sure you get the point across as to why an individual climber or your team should be sponsored.

- Address the letter to the sponsorship coordinator. Actually call the company and ask who this is. You don't need to speak with the sponsorship coordinator directly; he probably would rather you didn't until he has a letter and résumé on his desk that he can refer to.

- Begin the letter by stating an objective. Be specific but brief, an introduction. Also let the company know which of its products you enjoy using.

- The second paragraph should include information about what an individual or team can offer the sponsor. What do you have that will benefit the company you are contacting? Provide an irresistible reason to want to sponsor your team or an individual climber.

- The third paragraph includes what you want from the company, but do not be too specific. Companies sometimes have specific levels of sponsorship, and they do not waiver or negotiate. Tell the company you want to represent it by wearing or using its product.

- In the final paragraph, let the company know where you can be reached and thank the reader for her time.

- The letter should be limited to one page. Companies receive hundreds of letters each week, and the shorter the letter, the more likely it will be read.

Etiquette—Yours, Not Theirs

There is definitely a right and a wrong way to go about contacting companies. Once a letter and résumé have been sent, you do not need to call. Let the company contact you. An interested company will call immediately. If you have not heard from the company within two months, send an updated letter and résumé—be sure to add new accomplishments.

Again, *do not call* the company to ask if it has received your letter unless you have personally met the representative—and even then don't be a pest. When *can* you call? After you have updated your résumé at least two times over a period of approximately six months, you can call the rep and ask if the company has received your proposal.

If you talk to the representative at a trade show or competition, find out what the company wants from its sponsored athletes to see if you can meet those needs. This will save time and energy.

Have patience. It sometimes takes a significant amount of time to develop a relationship with a company. I once sent letters and updates to Aloe Up for more than a year; eventually I got one of the best contracts of my career.

At right is a sample letter to a potential sponsor. The items in italics must be included in your letter.

Sample Résumé Tips

- With an individual résumé, include a photo—close-up and climbing if possible. This will help put a name to a face.

- A team résumé should include a group photo, preferably of the team performing a service project.

- Write a brief description of the climber's individual goals: What does the climber want to accomplish, what kind of person is he. Give the company a picture of who the climber is.

Joe Doe Climber

512 Mount Hunter • Red Point, CO 80513 • 303–555–1212

September 10, 2002

Mr. Representative
Climbing Shoe Company X
777 On the Bay
Monterey, CA 88888

Dear Mr. Representative *(address the person with his title, not just a first name),*

After wearing my Zen's *(be specific and name the model)* for three years, I would like to pursue a more formal relationship with Climbing Shoe Company X as a sponsored athlete.

While wearing your shoes, I have competed in over twenty climbing competitions. My main focus is on USCCA competitions, but over the past year I have also been doing well in the ABS series. When I am not training and competing, I volunteer at the local climbing gym *(name the gym)* belaying beginner climbers. With my positive attitude, I feel I would be a good representative for Climbing Shoe Company X *(use the company name a few times).*

In exchange for my promotion of Climbing Shoe Company X, I would like to enter a sponsorship agreement with you.

Thank you for considering sponsoring me. I can be reached at the address or phone number above.

Sincerely,

Joe Doe Climber

Enclosure: résumé *(always include a résumé with the details of your climbing)*

Joe Doe Climber

Age: 17

USCCA ranking: 6th

ABS ranking: 15th

Redpoint level: 5.13b

Onsight level: 5.12c

Goals: My short-term goal is to increase my placing at USCCA events, so that I make the USCCA junior climbing team this season. Longterm, I would like to continue competing in ABS events so that I can make the U.S. Climbing Team and compete in World Cup events.

2002 Competition Results:

5th Place	Colorado Springs, CO	USCCA Regional Championship
3rd Place	Boulder, CO	USCCA Regional Championship
6th Place	Denver, CO	USCCA Regional Championship
5th Place	Philadelphia, PA	USCCA National Championship
10th Place	Boulder, CO	ABS Bouldering National Championship
6th Place	Fort Collins, CO	ABS Bouldering Local Championship

Redpoint and Onsight Routes:

5.13b redpoint	Red Rocks, NV	*The Sissy Traverse*
5.12c onsight	Red Rocks, NV	*Body English*
5.12c onsight	Estes Park, CO	*Weekend Warrior*
5.12c onsight	Boulder Canyon, CO	*Der Letze Zug*

Special Achievements:

Volunteering my time at the local climbing area to help cleanup has been rewarding. Not only do I feel like a part of the local climbing community, but I have also received media coverage in the local newspaper.

- Give a brief summary of competition finishes. Include only competitions in which the climber placed in the top five, unless it is a major competition such as a national or world event.

- Provide a brief summary of redpoint and onsight routes or boulder problems. In order to be considered for sponsorship, a young climber should be climbing a minimum of 5.13b/c for males, 5.12d/5.13a for females. Climbers wanting to be sponsored for bouldering alone should be climbing at least V10 for males and V7 for females.

- Include other things that will make the climber stand out, such as special projects and magazine articles/photos.

- Keep the résumé to only one page.

At left is a sample résumé.

Appendix

Glossary

Aerobic conditioning: Any activity to build up aerobic (lung) capacity. These activities can be biking, running, or in-line skating—any activity that brings up the heart rate.

Backstep/drop knee (technique): Turning one hip against the wall and using the outside edge of the back shoe to press on the foothold. The entire body is sideways against the wall, and the climber's inside arm is reaching for the next hold. If a climber is reaching upward with the right hand, the right outside edge is against the wall. *He saved valuable energy by backstepping that move.*

Barndoor (technique/bad): An out-of-balance position. A climber will usually have one hand and foot on the wall, then swing off, often facing away from the wall, appearing to "swing like a door on its hinges." This position uses energy as the climber has to fight the swing to get back into a balanced position.

Belay: The act of taking up rope as a climber ascends on the wall. A *belayer* is responsible for the safety of the climber and for lowering a climber off a route.

Belay device: Used by the belayer on the end of the rope opposite the climber. On TR the belayer takes up rope, feeding it through the belay device. When the climber reaches the top of the climb, the belayer lowers the climber to the ground by letting the rope feed through the belay device. Common belay devices include Grigri, Tuber, and ATC. A belay device can also be used to rappel off the top of a climb.

Beta (slang): Giving another climber advice or knowledge about a climb, or sharing information about how to do moves. *His beta was so good that I was able to flash the route.*

Body tension (technique): Pressing the body onto holds using the core muscles (center) of the body. Keeping equal pressure on all points of contact will keep the body from swinging off the holds. If a climber looses body tension, it can result in a fall. A pushup is a perfect example of "body tension"—tight abdominals keep the hips up.

Bolts and bolt hangers: A bolt holds a bolt hanger on either a climbing wall or natural rock. A sport climber leads up to the bolt hanger, clips a quick draw into it, and then clips the rope into the bottom carabiner.

Bomber (slang): A really good hold in a stable position. *The hold was so bomber, he was able to hang out on it for five minutes.* Term can also refer to the placement of traditional gear.

Bouldering (type): Climbing on boulders without using ropes. Usually the top of the boulder will be less than 20 feet high. Most boulder problems include only a few moves. Bouldering can also be done in a climbing gym.

Bowline: A common knot for tying the rope into the climber's harness.

Brain bucket (slang): Helmet used for climbing. Most climbers will not use a brain bucket while sport climbing or climbing in a gym. It is typically used during traditional climbing, ice climbing, and mountaineering but should be used in any outdoor climbing situation.

Bucket (hold): A large climbing hold that the climber can wrap his hand into. This hold can resemble a handlebar, and is very easy to hang on to.

Bump: To use a small, intermediate hold for balance before moving that same hand again. *She used a foothold to bump her right hand to the crimper.*

Campus (technique): To climb without using the feet. The climber will "lock off" with one arm and reach for the next hold with the other.

Campus board: Usually a piece of plywood attached to a frame so that it over-hangs with pieces of wood attached horizontally at equal intervals. A climber uses the wood as handholds. Feet are not used on a campus board.

Carabiner: A metal piece of equipment, which attaches the "belay device" to the harness of the belayer and is also attached on each end of a quick draw. A cara-biner is either oval or "D" shaped with a gate that opens to the inside. Carabiners used with the belay device have a lock—either a screw lock or automatic lock—that prevents it from accidentally opening. Carabiners are also used at the top of toproped climbs for the rope to run through.

Chalk: A substance (gymnastics chalk/magnesium sulfate) used by climbers to pre-vent "greasing" or "peeling" off holds. A climber will dip his hand into a chalk bag, then rub the chalk onto it to absorb sweat.

Chalk bag: A small cotton or nylon bag that holds chalk and is attached to the climber's waist with a piece of webbing. The climber will dip his hand into the bag to get chalk on his fingers.

Chalk ball: A small nylon bag with a drawstring that holds chalk. This "ball" is placed inside a chalk bag. A chalk ball will not spill if the chalk bag is dropped.

Contact strength: The ability to stick a hold with the fingers on immediate contact with a hold.

Crank (technique/slang): Pulling with the arms to get higher on a route. *She cranked through those moves without any trouble.*

Cross training: Refers to any activity used in conjunction with the primary sport. Running can be a cross training activity for climbing.

Crux (slang): The most difficult part of a climb, usually one or more moves that are at the climber's limit. *When she got to the crux she struggled through the moves.* Can also refer to the mental state of a climber—a crucial moment on a climb where the climber must make a decision to continue or to retreat.

Deadpoint (technique): A climber makes a move for a hold that looks as though it could be out of reach, but he is able to complete the move with his feet still on holds. The climber will be fully extended but have four points of contact.

Deck (slang): To hit the ground without the rope slowing down the climber. It is usually due to a bad belay or miscommunication.

Down climb: To reverse the moves on a climb and go from a high point down to a lower point on the route.

Draw (slang): A quick draw. A piece of webbing with a carabiner on each end.

Drop knee (technique): Also called a "backstep." Turning one hip against the wall so that the body is perpendicular to the wall and pushing with the outside edge of the climbing shoe. For example, if the climber needs to reach up with her left hand, her left hip will be pulled into the wall and the left outside edge of her climbing shoe will be on the hold. It is called a drop knee because it often looks as though the knee is pointing downward, toward the ground.

Dyno (technique): Short for "dynamic." When the climber loses all points of contact with the wall and continues an upward motion. This is done by pushing on the legs and pulling with the arms, letting go of the holds and "flying" upward to catch the next hand hold.

Edge (hold): A tiny climbing hold only big enough for the first digit (pad) of the fingers. Can also be a small sliver of a foothold, and is sometimes referred to as a "dime-sized edge."

Endurance: The body's ability to endure—usually means physical/muscular longevity. Endurance can also be a mental state.

Engrams: The muscles' ability to remember movement.

Figure-8 knot: The most common knot for tying the rope to the climber's harness. This knot looks like an "8" when tied correctly. For safety, after the figure-8 knot is tied into the rope and threaded through the harness, it is then "retraced" back through.

Flag (technique): Placing one foot out to the side of the body for balance, without touching a foothold. The foot will probably be touching the wall, sometimes with a bit of pressure to keep the climber from "barndooring" off the wall.

Flash (slang): To climb a route on the first attempt from the bottom to the top without a fall, but with having previous knowledge of the climb. *After learning about a no-hands rest halfway up the route, she flashed it without a problem.*

Flash pump: When climbing on hard routes too quickly, the forearms will become engorged with blood, and the muscles will tighten up. Sometimes a flash pump will remain during the rest of the session and not go away. The best way to get rid of a flash pump is to massage the area, stretch it, and take at least a twenty-minute rest to allow the muscles to cool down and the lactic acid to dissipate. After taking twenty minutes of rest, the climber should then warm up again, very slowly.

Free climbing (type): Climbing using only the body for upward movement. Not using any "aid" (ropes or gear) to pull the body up a climb. If a climber is "free climbing," he may be using gear to clip his rope into the rock, but he is only using his own movement on the rock to get higher on the climb.

Free soloing (type): Climbing without using any gear or ropes. Only extremely experienced climbers should do this type of climbing. Because there is no safety gear to catch the climber, any fall can result in death.

Gaston (hold): A hold that is held with the palm facing away from the climber. The climber pushes sideways (and usually down) on the hold with his fingers.

Gear: Refers to equipment a climber uses as protection during a climb. In traditional climbing, this includes pitons (pieces of metal pounded into the rock), nuts (removable pieces of metal that are placed in cracks), and friends (removable pieces of metal that expand and contract to fit all sizes of cracks). In sport climbing, gear is bolts and bolt hangers (permanently attached to the rock) and quick draws.

Grease (slang): To have a hand or foot come off a hold. This can happen in hot and/or humid conditions when the holds become "greasy" or slick because of sweat. *Her foot greased off the hold and she took a huge fall.*

Hang: To sit with weight on the rope. If a climber is "hanging," he is probably resting with his entire body weight in his harness and not climbing upward.

Harness: The sewn webbing a climber wears around her waist and legs. A climber chooses a harness that is snug, but not tight. If a climber falls, the harness will absorb some of the impact of the fall.

Hold: What a climber uses on an indoor, artificial wall or outdoors on real rock to hold onto with the hands and feet. Holds in a climbing gym may be marked with colored tape to designate a route up the wall, but outdoors a climber must figure out holds on his own.

Intermediate (hold): A small hold that a climber probably can't use to actually move off but will use to help get the body into a better position to get to the next hold.

Jug (hold): A large climbing hold that a climber can typically hold with an entire hand. Very easy to hold on to; also called a "bucket."

Lead climbing (type): A type of climbing in which the climber gets to the top of the climb using gear or quick draws to clip in the rope as she ascends. When lead climbing in a climbing gym, quick draws are hanging from bolt hangers on the wall. The climber starts at the bottom and clips the rope into the quick draws as she climbs up the wall. If a climber falls when sport climbing, the quick draw and belayer will "catch" her fall.

Lie back (technique): The feet and hands are facing the same direction, with the side of the body against the rock. Upward movement is made by putting pressure on the feet and then moving the hands up the rock.

Lock off (technique): Pulling up with one arm so that the elbow is bent. The forearm and biceps are probably touching. This technique is used when reaching for a hold.

Match (technique): Putting both hands or feet on a single hold.

Mono (hold): A "pocket" into which only one finger will fit. Can be deep enough to accept the entire finger or shallow to accept only the pad of the finger.

Negatives: Reversing a move—the opposite of pulling up, it is lowering the body down (from a lock off to a straight arm). Negatives are used as a training tool, often on a systems board.

Onsight (slang): To climb a route without having any previous knowledge of the climb. Onsight climbing refers to the first attempt on a route. If previous knowledge of a climb exists, it is a "flash."

Overall conditioning: Building up all aspects of climbing—endurance, power, and power-endurance—gradually during a training cycle.

Overhang: A climbing wall or rock that is farther away at the top than at the base. If a climber is facing the climbing wall at the base, she would have to tilt her head back to see the top of the wall.

Pedaling (slang): The movement of a speed climber's feet. The climber will be looking up for handholds, letting his feet land on holds without looking at them. The legs look as though they are pedaling a bicycle.

Peel (slang): To come off a hold and usually fall off the route. One or more points of contact (hand or foot) break contact with the holds. *His right hand peeled off the hold unexpectedly and he took a 20-foot whipper.*

Pinch (hold): A climbing hold that must be held with the fingers on one side and the thumb on the other. Pinches can vary in size from small (just fingertips on the hold) to large (entire hand wrapped around).

Pocket (hold): A climbing hold that the climber can put his fingers, and some-times his entire hand into. Pockets vary in size from a mono (single-finger pocket) to two-finger pockets to jugs and can vary in depth, from single digit to entire finger.

Points of contact (slang): Refers to the number of body parts (hands and feet) touching the wall. Technical climbers strive for three points of contact—moving only one hand or foot at a time. When a climber does a "dyno," she has zero points of contact.

Power: A quick motion, usually involving full muscular strength and momentum. The development of power helps climbers complete difficult moves.

Power-endurance: The use of endurance in difficult climbing situations—more sustained climbing than endurance and easier moves than power.

Power spot: To physically push a climber through a move. Power spotting can help a climber learn a move (body position) before trying it on his own. Builds a climber's confidence to do the move on his own.

Protection/pro (slang): A piece of gear or equipment that is placed in the rock to catch a climber in the event of a fall. Protection/gear is either placed in a crack or clipped to a bolt hanger.

Pumped (slang): Lactic acid buildup in the forearms, causing fatigue in the muscles. *He was so pumped from that climb that he could pound nails with his forearms.*

Quick draw: A quick draw consists of three components. It is a piece of sewn webbing with a carabiner attached to each end. The climber attaches the quick draws to his harness to attach on the way up a lead climb, or the quick draws will already be hanging on the wall, attached to a bolt hanger for the climber to clip the lead climbing rope through on the way to the top of the wall.

Redpoint: To complete a climb with no falls on a subsequent effort after the first attempt.

Roof: An overhanging climbing wall or rock. It can be a continuous overhang, such as 25 degrees overhanging, or different angles, with a horizontal roof at any point on the wall. The degree of the overhang can also refer to the distance the wall overhangs from the bottom to the top. *The roof overhangs 25 feet in 60 feet of climbing.*

Rope: Most climbers use dynamic rope, which stretches during impact or a fall. Static line is rope that does not stretch and is used primarily for toprope climbing and rappelling.

Route (slang): An actual climb, including all holds and features that will be used. *The route took a circuitous path to the top of the wall.*

Sandbag: To tell someone a route is easier than it actually is. *He said this route was a 5.10, but it was actually a 5.11+—I was sandbagged!*

Send (slang): To complete a climb from the bottom to the top without falling. *She was able to send the route on her fourth attempt.*

Shoes: Climbing shoes are specifically designed to stick to rock and artificial climbing holds. They should fit tightly and have a "sticky" rubber sole. Climbers will wear their climbing shoes two to four sizes smaller than their street shoes. A tight fit is essential in technical climbing so that a climber can feel the holds through the rubber.

Short roped (slang): When the belayer has the rope so tight that it prohibits movement by the climber. This can be done either on toprope or lead. On toprope, the rope would essentially pull the climber up the wall—and sometimes off the wall if it is overhanging. On lead, being short roped can prohibit upward movement by the climber.

Sidepull (hold): A hold that faces away from the climber. The climber would pull sideways on the hold with his fingers.

Slab: A rock that is not vertical, but leans away from the climber, like a ladder leaning against a building. To climb a slab, the climber must use friction to stand on her feet, as the holds can be rather small. A climber should attempt to stand straight up and not lean into the rock on a slab.

Sloper (hold): A climbing hold that resembles the bottom of a rounded bowl. A sloper causes the climber to use an open-handed grip and skin friction to grip the hold.

Speed climbing (type): Getting to the top of the climb as quickly as possible. This type of climbing is done outside on large walls, such as El Capitan and Half Dome in Yosemite. In competitions, climbers are on toprope for protection and speed.

Sport climbing (type): Lead climbing using bolt hangers and quick draws for protection. Bolt hangers are strategically placed permanently on the rock. The climber clips a quick draw into a bolt hanger, and the rope is then clipped into the bottom carabiner of the quick draw, protecting the climber in case of a fall.

Straight on (technique): The position of the climber in relation to the climbing surface. The shoulders and hips are facing the climbing wall. *Climbing the route straight on saved him valuable time.*

Systems training: A methodical approach to training that encompasses strengthening the body in a balanced way. When systems training, a climber will work the right and left sides of the body so that all positions are equal. If a climber is weaker on the right side than on the left in any particular movement, she can work that side until it is equally strong.

Take!: A term of communication from the climber to the belayer used when a climber does not want to take a fall or is too tired to make a move. Saying "take" will spur the belayer to take up the slack in the rope. Also used when the climber reaches the top of a climb and wants the belayer to take up the slack before lowering.

Throw (slang): To physically throw the body toward a climbing hold. The climber's hips are the generating force of motion in "throwing" for a hold. The movement originates in the legs, the hips are pressed forward, and the momentum carries the climber upward.

Toprope/TR (type): When the rope is attached to the top of the wall, the climber ties into the rope at the bottom. The climber is protected by the rope above her and by the belayer taking up the opposite end of the rope as the climber moves up the wall.

Topping out: Reaching the top of a climb.

Traditional climbing (type): Lead climbing while placing gear. "Trad" climbing is usually done in cracks, where removable gear will fit into the slot of a crack to protect the climber in the event of a fall. The climber must carry an assortment of gear to fit into any opening of the crack.

Training to peak: A style of training where the climber works on endurance for approximately one month, then works on power-endurance, and then power. Each aspect is worked on exclusively, and at the end of the cycle, the climber should "peak."

Traverse (technique): The act of moving sideways (horizontally) on the climbing surface.

Tufa (hold): A long, skinny climbing hold resembling a stalactite from a cave. Mostly found in humid, limestone areas but also replicated as artificial climbing holds.

Turnout: Refers to the flexibility of the hip joint and how far the knees can rotate to the outside of the body with the knees bent.

Whipper (slang): A fall where the climber is caught by the rope.

Resources

Advanced Rock Climbing, John Long and Craig Leubben (Falcon, 1997). Straightforward information on face climbing, crack climbing, equipment, anchors, belaying, rappelling, sport climbing, etc. A great resource for climbing outdoors!

Athlete's Guide to Sponsorship, Jennifer Drury and Cheri Elliott (Velo Press, 1998). Not specifically intended for rock climbing but a great reference nonetheless. Excellent advice for teams and individuals.

Better Bouldering, John Sherman (Falcon, 1997). A high-quality book. "Painfully objective." Fun and informative, just like John himself.

Bouldering with Bobbi Bensman, Bobbi Bensman (Stackpole, 1999). A bouldering guide with basic to advanced moves.

Climbing Anchors, John Long (Falcon, 1993). An excellent source to read before climbing outdoors. There are tips on fixed anchors, traditional equipment, equalizing protection, etc.

Climbing Your Best: Training to Maximize Your Performance, Heather Reynolds Sagar (Stackpole, 2001). Heather Sagar is a professional climbing trainer and coach. This book includes strategies for overcoming psychological barriers, exercises, and programs for improving strength, flexibility, and technique. Also included are tests for assessing personal strengths and weaknesses.

Climbing: A Woman's Guide, Shelley Presson (Ragged Mountain, 2000). A comprehensive beginner's guide aimed at female climbers. This book takes you through the basics to beginner and intermediate techniques. It also covers equipment and safety. Good all around climbing reference.

Fingers of Steel (video), Tony Yaniro (Excalibur Distribution). One of the best training videos I have ever seen. Explanations are easy to understand, with humor thrown in to lighten things up.

Flash Training, Eric Hörst (Falcon, 1994). An excellent guide for training strength, technique, mental, etc. Although it is not a book you can just sit down and read, the suggestions and tips are by far some of the best available.

How to Rock Climb!, John Long (Falcon, 1998). A basic and comprehensive book to the sport.

Performance Rock Climbing, Dale Goddard and Udo Neumann (Stackpole, 1993). Although not quite as good as *Flash Training*, it is an excellent training guide with excessive explanations. There is also a video available for those who don't like to read.

Thinking Body, Dancing Mind, Chungliang Al Huang (Bantam, 1992). You won't find this book in the climbing section, but it is one of the best sources for mental training.

Toproping, Peter Lewis (Falcon, 1998). A great reference for making the transition from indoor to outdoor climbing. This book will give you everything you need to know to set up topropes, belay, and climb on toprope outdoors.

Programs and Organizations

USCCA (FORMERLY JCCA AND ASCF)

The United States Competition Climbing Association, or USCCA (the combined American Sport Climbers Federation and Junior Competition Climbing Association), ranks junior climbers—any climber under nineteen years of age. Since changing their name in 2002, the USCCA includes adults as well as young climbers. The USCCA has a series of competitions in climbing gyms all over the United States. Competitors must earn points to go from regionals to regional championships, to divisionals, and on to nationals. The U.S. Junior Climbing Team is selected from the Junior National Competition. This team consists of the top four climbers in each age division. Members of the Junior Climbing Team can compete in the Youth World Championship, which is held annually in locations all over the world.

The USCCA has two types of competitions at the regional level—redpoint and bouldering. At the national level, the competitions are onsight format, as is the Youth World event.

Membership in the USCCA starts at $40 per year.

USCCA, P.O. Box 502568, Indianapolis, IN 46250
(888) 788–5222
www.usclimbing.org

ABS

The American Bouldering Series (ABS) holds competitions in climbing gyms all over the United States and Canada. In 2002 there were more than one hundred grass-root bouldering competitions in forty states. These competitions are mainly fun, informal events, but in 2001 the ABS started hosting a national level bouldering event, attracting top climbers from around the world.

ABS, P.O. Box 3710, Boulder, CO 80307
(888) 944–4244
www.rockcomps.com

Youth climbers on the wall at a European onsight competition in Imst, Austria. Photo: Craig Axtell

WORLD YOUTH

The World Youth Competition takes place once per year, in a different location each summer or fall. Competitors must be invited to participate in this event and must be at least fourteen years of age. Check out the results from this year's event at www.digitalrock.de.

U.S. JUNIOR CLIMBING TEAM

The top four climbers in each USCCA age division will be selected for the U.S. Junior Climbing Team. Those climbers will have the opportunity to attend the Junior World Competition.

U.S. ADULT CLIMBING AND BOULDERING TEAMS

The U.S. Climbing and Bouldering Teams consist of the top eight climbers—male and female—at the USCCA Onsight National and Bouldering National. The top four climbers are considered the "A" team, and the next four climbers are the "B" team. Members of the U.S. Climbing Team receive a team jacket and are eligible to compete at world cup events (mainly in Europe).

The 2001 U.S. Junior Team in Imst, Austria, at the Junior World Championship. Photo: Craig Axtell

Index

About the Author

Michelle Hurni began climbing in 1980. In 1992 she turned professional, competing all around the world. From 1993 to 2000 she held an honored position on the U.S. Climbing Team and was ranked the number-one overall female climber during the 1998–99 season.

In 1998 Michelle founded the U.S. Climbing Team Junior Pro Camps and directed and instructed more than thirty students for three years during the camps' two-week sessions. To pass along the knowledge that was given to her during her years of competitive climbing, Michelle started giving "Beyond the Basics" clinics for women around the United States, an experience that led to this book, *Coaching Climbing*. While not climbing, Michelle writes for the ESPN X Games and for publications such as *Rock & Ice*.